THE LITTLE
BLACK BOOK OF
BUSINESS
MATH

THE LITTLE
BLACK BOOK OF
BUSINESS
MATH

Michael C. Thomsett

amacom
American Management Association

This book is available at a special
discount when ordered in bulk quantities.
For information, contact Special Sales Department,
AMACOM, a division of American Management Association,
135 West 50th Street, New York, NY 10020.

Library of Congress Cataloging-in-Publication Data

Thomsett, Michael C.
   The little black book of business math.

   Includes index.
   1. Business mathematics. I. Title. II. Title:
Business math.
HF5691.T48   1988   513'.93   87-37360
ISBN 0-8144-7691-0

Printing number

10 9 8 7 6 5 4 3 2 1

To
my
brother,
Peter R. Thomsett

Contents

Introduction

"I have hardly ever known a mathematician who was capable of reasoning."

—Plato

A marketing department supervisor was training a new employee. After an hour of explaining exactly how a particularly complex monthly report was to be prepared, she suggested that the math should be checked with a calculator. "That way, you'll be sure you have the correct answer," she explained.

"Okay," the confused employee responded, "but can you tell me once again, what was the question?"

The easiest and most widely used method for measuring results and reporting information is mathematical. How much profit? How many units? What rate of production? All calculations require the expression of results in numerical form. In business we all must use several applications of math: statistical reporting, financial analysis, return calculations, and interpretation of performance results, for instance.

However, many people have trouble with the process of resolving math problems, a struggle that may go back to high school. Actually, it is not the manipulation of numbers that gives most people trouble, but the decision about which numbers to manipulate. We must understand which questions to ask before we can develop the right solution. The hard part is developing the power to reason.

This book is a summary of the most common forms of measure-

1

ment that you are asked to use. It will lead you through the methods of calculation, explain the reasoning, and provide examples. At the end of each chapter, a number of work project questions are included so that you may test your grasp of the subject. Answers and explanations are provided in the appendix.

The purpose of this book is to reduce the common business applications of math to a level that you can use in your job. You will gain math comfort step by step, and with it the personal confidence to tackle a table, chart, report, or analysis that previously left you confused or frustrated. You'll learn how to define a problem, how to break it down into logical and simple components, and explain your conclusions with clarity. You will discover that math is not so mysterious or complicated that it cannot be mastered. And with that mastery will come a sense of confidence and personal accomplishment.

Keep this little black book in a desk drawer, hidden beneath a stack of files or disguised as an expense record. If you want to make certain that no one else finds this book in your possession, some experts recommend using a plain brown book cover, marked "Procedures." Take the book out when you're confronted with a math challenge; you'll get your answers in an instant. This book will help you succeed with one of the most important skills there is—being able to explain complex information in clear, concise, and understandable form.

1

Defining the Problem

"It is better to know some of the questions than all of the answers."

—James Thurber

"How do you solve a problem?" the young job applicant was asked.

"Well, first of all," she said, "I'd have to understand what the problem was."

She was hired on the spot.

The only way to master math is to become an expert in defining the problem. Real-world problems—even math problems—are not presented in neat rows and columns, requiring simple addition or subtraction. You are given facts and asked to develop the right questions on your own. Knowing how to solve is a two-step process. First, you must understand the problem. Then you apply the math skills needed to derive an answer.

Numbers themselves have no real meaning; it is the value underlying the numbers that you must comprehend—the significance of facts in relation to one another, and the way those facts are expressed and communicated in the solving process. Before you can succeed with that, you must be able to get the essential information, arrange it, and use it in the most appropriate way. So the real problem comes down to approaching and visualizing the question, *before* undertaking the solution. What we need is a logical and ordered technique for the expression of information using mathematical facts. See "The Steps in a Solution."

The Steps in a Solution

1. Get *all* the facts you need to solve the problem. Know what variables must be allowed for, and verify the accuracy of what you're told.
2. Test the assumption. If, for example, you are told that there is no seasonal variation in sales statistics, check the actual numbers. You may discover that, while sales activity doesn't vary, there is a predictable trend in when those sales hit the books.
3. Adjust the assumptions to match the facts.
4. Decide the best method for calculating the right answer.
5. Review your results. Does your answer appear realistic? If not, check your assumptions and the method you used in applying them to your calculation.

THE FUNDAMENTAL CONCEPTS

One reason so many people struggle with math is that, while they were busy learning the basics, they never understood how it would ever apply to them. If you work in an administrative capacity, for instance, how often do you use square roots? Or compute pi? Yet as a student, you were expected to be able to do all the various calculations, often without a grounding in the theory itself. In that respect, education has failed many people. Being forced to master a technique without an explanation of why and when that skill will be used is the most difficult form of learning. It is always easier to develop skills if we know why we may need them.

The typical schoolbook question goes something like this: "Billy had four apples. John had six. And Mark had eight more. How many apples did the three boys have in all?" This is not so much a test of addition ability as a test of reasoning. The best way to learn how to do these kinds of problems is to visualize—actually picture the three boys, with their apples. Once you begin to do that, the abstract narrative problem can be solved.

As you have probably discovered by now, you are called upon to use some math functions in your job, and they often involve the same types of calculations that you were asked to solve in school. Just like the three boys with the apples, the business assignments involving computation require correct visual understanding if they are to be solved correctly. But instead of being provided everything you need to solve the problem, you're usually given little to go on at the start. In business, the problem about the three boys and the apples might come to you like this: "Analyze this apple thing. Find out who has them, how many they have, and what they're doing with them. Then see if there's a way they can get by with less apples than they're using now."

DEFINE THE PROBLEM

Rarely does the boss present you with a page of problems and ask for calculated answers. More than likely, you are expected to develop methods on your own, which is much more difficult than the actual math.

Let's suppose your boss has asked you to develop a sales forecast for next year. The marketing department advises you that each sales division will expect an 8% increase in field staff, and that average volume per person will rise 11% for the year.

What do you know from the information you have?

1. The numbers will go up for the year.
2. The forecast will be based on previous volume.
3. Both the number of staff in the field and the average volume per salesperson will rise.

First you'll need to gather certain facts:

1. Present sales levels.
2. The number of people in the field staff.

The problem cannot be solved without that basic information. Too often, in fact, we are asked to report without adequate information. The result is faulty reporting, based on incorrect or even nonexistent assumptions. This cannot always be blamed on the individual preparing the report. But you realize that you need this information, so you do the necessary research and discover:

1. There are now 500 salespeople.
2. Total sales volume last year was $36 million.

Now you must compute the average sales volume generated per salesperson during the past year, because one of the assumptions (11% increase) is expressed as a per-person average and you need all operating facts in the same format. Visualize 500 people out in the field, all selling their share per month. If total volume of sales last year was $36 million, then each person averaged $72,000 for the year ($36 million divided by 500).

Remember, numbers by themselves have little meaning. To be valid, the calculations you go through must be based on solid information and a clear understanding of what you want to accomplish—what the real problem is. You have been told the sales force will increase by 8% next year, and that average volume per person will grow by 11%. An 8% increase in a sales force of 500 is 40 additional people. If you assume recruiting will occur throughout the year, that's an average of 3 1/3 new people per month. Obviously, you can apply the 11% increase only to the existing sales force, those who were around last year. You'll have to use last year's average as this year's forecast for the new people. So a logical way to proceed is to separate monthly figures into two groups, one for the existing sales force and one for new people.

Prepare the Forecast

Start by listing the facts you have at hand:

Existing sales force:	
Number of people	500
Average volume last year	$72,000
11% increase this year ($72,000 × 1.11, rounded up)	$80,000
Monthly average	$ 6,667

New sales recruits:
Number of people (8% increase over 500
current) 40
Average new recruits per month 3 1/3
Annual volume (based on last year) $72,000
Monthly average $ 6,000

At this point, you have the numbers of people, the anticipated volume each, and some preliminary assumptions about the timing of volume and recruiting. This example is too complex to compute in one step. You have an increase in average volume, an increase in the sales force itself, different standards for estimating per-person production, and the possibility of seasonal variation. It is likely that most business problems will be complex, with a number of variables to consider. In such cases, attack the problem by breaking it down into smaller parts.

Also, there's a lot you don't know yet. Some questions you should ask to ensure that your forecast will be accurate:

1. Does the 8% increase represent a gross number, or are some members of the current sales force also expected to resign? If attrition is expected, how much will it be? The answer will affect your calculations.

2. Will all salespeople experience increases of 11%? Or will that apply only to the current sales force, with new people expected to perform at a lower level? If so, for how long?

3. Are there seasonal considerations? For example, will the majority of new people come on board early in the year, late in the year, or evenly throughout? Will total sales be greater at one time of the year than another?

It's possible you might find concrete answers to those questions. But more likely, you'll have to use some assumptions—after all, this is a forecast into the future, with some unknowns. A good sound way to approach this is to make your best logical guess about these unknowns, and then go over it with your boss.

CLARIFY ASSUMPTIONS AND METHOD

The forecast of next year's sales could be prepared in a number of ways. With shallow assumptions, it will be far less accurate than it will be with more detailed information at hand. Let's say you're not sure whether your method will produce dependable results. Gather your source information, list your assumptions, and write down the procedure you intend to use. Then meet with your boss and present what you have. Ask for approval of the procedure before going ahead with it, or for modifications.

Your presentation can consist of a very concise set of facts and assumptions, such as:

Marketing assumptions:
    8% increase in sales force
    11% increase in average revenues
Historical facts:
    Current sales force, 500
    Average production, $72,000
Forecast assumptions:
    Increases in average production will apply only to existing sales
        force personnel; for new recruits last year's average will be
        used.
    The 8% increase is over and above any expected terminations.
    There will be no variance for seasonal change, either in sales volume
        or recruiting.
    Production for new recruits should be estimated to begin 90 days
        after recruitment date.

Your boss may suggest some modifications, such as:
    ▪ Reduce current sales force estimates by three people per month, and estimate new-recruit volume by an additional three people per month (this will take care of the attrition factor). Also assume that on average, two new recruits hired each month will leave the company after six months.
    ▪ Calculate the volume increase for the existing sales force on a gradual level, not all at once, to realistically estimate the likely growth in sales. The level may not actually reach 11% growth until late in the year.
    This second change will make a substantial difference. Assuming 11% growth all year produces an average volume of $79,920. Assuming 1% per month for 11 months will result in a forecast of approximately $6,375 per month, or $76,500 for the year.

Presenting the method under which you intend to proceed gives you several advantages:

- It saves time and work by giving your supervisor the chance to modify the way you'll proceed.
- It improves communication, giving your supervisor confidence in your professionalism.
- If your assumptions are flawed, your supervisor can correct you before you prepare a report. This is preferable to errors being discovered after you have spent a lot of time on a project.

There is no fault in being wrong, as long as you give your supervisor the opportunity to train you before you spend a lot of company time struggling with a process; as long as you learn from the experience; and as long as you keep the lines of communication open. Don't assume that lack of knowledge itself will be criticized. The only time there is really a problem is when you fail to admit lack of knowledge, or proceed without fully understanding what you are doing.

If you use this technique for defining the problem (before you try to solve it), and communicate with your supervisor, you'll find the mathematical segments of your job more of a successful experience. Ultimately, the procedure will also add to your professional reputation.

PREPARE INFORMATION FOR VARIOUS AUDIENCES

Understanding the audience that will review your information means putting down your conclusions in the best possible format. An account-ant may be satisfied with a list of numbers, while a sales manager will prefer pie charts and comparative results. The president of the company may require a report with little or no details, with the essential informa-tion explained in narrative form.

Let's assume you are asked to provide results of your project to three different groups:

1. The accounting department, for inclusion in the forecast and budget for the entire company.

2. A budget review committee consisting of department managers.
3. The president.

The needs of each group are different, and you must prepare your report in three separate formats to satisfy each. A few ground rules for presenting similar information to different groups:

1. Make sure all information supplied on the different versions agrees *exactly* with that given on other formats.
2. The most extensive version of the report should be the one that is backed up with your documentation, regardless of where it's going.
3. It is helpful to explain that there are different versions available of the same report, and sometimes to back up a report with those other versions. For example, the president may want a two-sentence summary, but could also want to look at the detail.

Accounting Version: *Cover Memo*

Enclosed is the summary forecast of revenues for the coming year. Also enclosed are worksheets and assumption explanations.

A summarized version of this report was forwarded to the president's office, and a detailed version with assumptions was forwarded to the budget review committee.

Accounting Version: *The Report*

Total Sales per Month

Month	Sales	Month	Sales
Jan	$3,011,800	Jul	$ 3,225,200
Feb	3,023,300	Aug	3,270,500
Mar	3,034,400	Sep	3,321,400
Apr	3,081,100	Oct	3,354,000
May	3,127,500	Nov	3,386,200
Jun	3,179,500	Dec	3,396,200
		Total	$38,411,100

Accounting Version: *Supporting Material*

Include the full report sent to the budget review committee (detailed assumptions and worksheets for monthly totals).

Budget Committee Version: *Cover Memo*

Enclosed is the proposed forecast for revenues during the coming year.

The report includes a complete explanation of all assumptions that were incorporated into the forecast.

Two summarized versions of this information are being forwarded to the accounting department and president's office.

Budget Committee Version: *The Report*

A. Existing sales force
   1. Number of salespeople, assuming attrition of 3 per month from current level of 500.

Month	Number	Less	Net
Jan	500	3	497
Feb	497	3	494
Mar	494	3	491
Apr	491	3	488
May	488	3	485
Jun	485	3	482
Jul	482	3	479
Aug	479	3	476
Sep	476	3	473
Oct	473	3	470
Nov	470	3	467
Dec	467	3	464

   2. Monthly volume per person, assuming 1% increase in average per month, for 11 months.

Month	Volume	Month	Volume
Jan	$6,060	Jul	$6,420
Feb	6,120	Aug	6,480
Mar	6,180	Sep	6,540
Apr	6,240	Oct	6,600
May	6,300	Nov	6,660
Jun	6,360	Dec	6,660

3. Total revenues

Month	People	Monthly Volume	Total ($000)
Jan	497	$6,060	$ 3,011.8
Feb	494	6,120	3,023.3
Mar	491	6,180	3,034.4
Apr	488	6,240	3,045.1
May	485	6,300	3,055.5
Jun	482	6,360	3,065.5
Jul	479	6,420	3,075.2
Aug	476	6,480	3,084.5
Sep	473	6,540	3,093.4
Oct	470	6,600	3,102.0
Nov	467	6,660	3,110.2
Dec	464	6,660	3,090.2
		Total	$36,791.1

B. New recruits
   1. Number of recruits is based upon assumed increase over last year of 8% (40 new people, or 3.3 per month), plus additional three per month before attrition; it is also assumed that two recruits will terminate per month, beginning six months after hire date.

Month	Beginning Count	Plus Recruits	Less Attrition	Ending Count
Jan	0	6	0	6
Feb	6	6	0	12
Mar	12	7	0	19
Apr	19	6	0	25
May	25	6	0	31
Jun	31	7	0	38
Jul	38	6	2	42
Aug	42	6	2	46
Sep	46	7	2	51
Oct	51	6	2	55
Nov	55	6	2	59
Dec	59	7	2	64

   2. Monthly volume per person is based upon last year's average of $6,000; for new recruits, a 90-day delay is assumed for volume to be booked.

Month	People	Volume	Total ($000)	Month Booked
Jan	6	$6,000	$ 36	Apr
Feb	12	6,000	72	May
Mar	19	6,000	114	Jun
Apr	25	6,000	150	Jul
May	31	6,000	186	Aug
Jun	38	6,000	228	Sep
Jul	42	6,000	252	Oct
Aug	46	6,000	276	Nov
Sep	51	6,000	306	Dec
Oct	55	6,000		
Nov	59	6,000		
Dec	64	6,000		
		Total	$1,620	

C. Total volume

	Total Volume		
Month	Existing ($000)	New ($000)	Total ($000)
Jan	$ 3,011.8	$ 0.0	$ 3,011.8
Feb	3,023.3	0.0	3,023.3
Mar	3,034.4	0.0	3,034.4
Apr	3,045.1	36.0	3,081.1
May	3,055.5	72.0	3,127.5
Jun	3,065.5	114.0	3,179.5
Jul	3,075.2	150.0	3,225.2
Aug	3,084.5	186.0	3,270.5
Sep	3,093.4	228.0	3,321.4
Oct	3,102.0	252.0	3,354.0
Nov	3,110.2	276.0	3,386.2
Dec	3,090.2	306.0	3,396.2
Total	$36,791.1	$1,620.0	$38,411.1

Budget Committee Version: *Supporting Material*

Assumptions used to prepare next year's forecast of sales volume:

1. Increases in sales force: estimated at 8% for the year, net of attrition.

2. Attrition: existing sales force, 3 per month; new recruits, 2 per month beginning six months from date of hire.
3. Average volume, existing sales force: based on last year's average of $6,000 per person, existing sales force will increase 11% for the year, computed at 1% per month for 11 months.
4. New recruit volume: this is forecast at last year's average volume level, and a 90-day delay is assumed from hire date to volume being booked.

President's Version: *Cover Memo*

Enclosed is a summary of the forecast of revenues for the coming year.

Also enclosed is a copy of the more detailed reports forwarded to the budget review committee and to the accounting department.

President's Version: *The Report*

A conservative level of growth is being forecast for the coming year, based upon management's belief that our rate of volume and average production per salesperson will not continue to grow at the recent established rate. We estimate an increase of 6.7% over last year's volume of $36 million, compared with a previous year's growth level of 9%.

Net increase in the sales force is predicted along a trend established in the past, with 28 new salespeople by the end of the year (64 new people less attrition of 36). It is estimated that average gross volume per year will grow by $764 per person, compared with growth last year of more than $2,000, based on total production divided by the number of salespeople.

In summary:

	2 Years Ago	1 Year Ago	Estimated Next Year
Sales force	474	500	528
Total sales ($000)	$33,016	$35,992	$38,411
% increase	—	9.0%	6.7%
Average sales per person	$69,654	$71,984	$72,748

President's Version: Supporting Material

Include copies of the complete reports sent to the accounting department and to the budget review committee.

KEY POINTS

- A solution can be right only if you have all the facts, and base your calculations on dependable information.
- There may be more than one right or acceptable answer. In our forecasting example, your method may result in an answer that is much different from someone else's, but both approaches may be valid and acceptable.
- Calculations and assumptions must be documented. In most business reporting and communicating that involves math, the need for proof is ever-present. For example, a conclusion based on a set of assumptions should be supported by the narrative description of your process as well as by the computations themselves. Be prepared to explain how you arrived at the answer. In a management review, someone will invariably ask, "Where do these numbers come from?" Too often, the question gets a complicated answer and a number of worksheets. Or someone admits, "We based them on last year's averages." Somewhere in between is a crisp, clear, professional explanation. That is what you should strive to provide.

What if your answer appears to be way out of line? If sales last year were $36 million, and your forecast comes out to more than $800 million, with only an 11% increase per salesperson, something is obviously wrong. At that point, you must review your assumptions and calculation method. Always check your own conclusions before turning in the final document. Don't submit to your boss information that contains obvious mistakes.

- Some people are intimidated by math challenges because (1) they are afraid of being criticized for turning in faulty work, and (2) they are overwhelmed by the complexity of a problem.

On the first point: If you are diligent in the method and research you put into defining a problem, you will be recognized as conscientious. You cannot be criticized as long as you apply that philosophy in the process of solving a problem. On the second point: Complex problems are made simple when broken down into logical component parts. The thought of reading an 800-page book is exhausting, but you can easily handle one chapter at a time.

WORK PROJECT

1. Your company's forecast for future revenues is to be based on average production per salesperson. Prepare a forecast based on the following facts. Use the format suggested in the "Forecasting" and "Assumptions" worksheets to compute this answer and the answer to Question 2.

   (1) Assume that of a current force of 366, an average of 3 people per month will leave the company.

   (2) Last year, the sales average per person was $91,200 for the year.

   (3) Estimate growth in average production for existing salespeople at the rate of 1.5% per month.

   (4) New recruits will be added on an average of 4 people per month.

   (5) Of new recruits, half will leave the company six months after being hired.

   (6) Estimate new-recruit production at 50% of last year's average per person.

   (7) Assume production for new recruits will not hit the books until three months after hire month.

2. Alter your computation of revenues in question 1 for the following variables:

   (8) A seasonal slowdown of 5% of total revenues, affecting the ninth through twelfth months.

   (9) An increase in new-recruit production of 1% per month beginning in the seventh month after hire date.

forecasting worksheet

	MONTH:
Existing sales force (A)	
Less: attrition (B)	
Sales force after attrition (C)	
Average production (D)	
TOTAL SALES	
New recruits (E)	
Less: attrition (F)	
New recruits after attrition	
Average production (G)	
TOTAL SALES	
TOTAL ALL SALES	
Seasonal adjustment (H).	
New recruit adjustment (I)	
ADJUSTED TOTAL SALES	

assumptions

A _____

_____

B _____

_____

C _____

_____

D _____

_____

E _____

_____

F _____

_____

G _____

_____

H _____

_____

I _____

_____

2

Converting Values

"It's not what you pay a man but what he costs you that counts."

—Will Rogers

The reporter wrote: "The incidence of deliberately set fires has increased 900% in the last 15 years." One editor suggested changing the statistic to read, "There are nine arson fires today for every one 15 years ago," but the writer fought the change. He stubbornly insisted, "That's not accurate. Fires have gone up 900%, not 9 to 1."

Once you master the processes of defining problems and communicating with your supervisor, you have overcome the greatest hurdle to understanding business math. But the way information is developed is not always the most appropriate form for communication to others. It must often be converted to something better. Also, frequently you will need to make a conversion before you begin your computations, because you are not always supplied data in the most usable form.

Conversion means changing an expression of value from one form to another. The three forms in common use are fractions, percentages, and decimals. Business statistics may be stated in any one of the forms and often require conversion to another. For example, the fact that average volume per salesperson is expected to increase by 8% could be expressed

as a percentage: an 8% increase.
as a decimal: an increase of .08 times.
as a fraction: a 1/12 higher level.

CHOOSE THE BEST FORM

The mechanics of conversion—from decimals to fractions, from percentages to decimals—are fairly simple to master; this chapter will show you how. The finesse comes in deciding which form is most appropriate for a particular audience. For example, how would you best express information in a narrative report to management? Let's say you have calculated that cost-control efforts have resulted in a 25% decrease in telephone expenses over a three-month period. Which of the following best communicates this?

1. Telephone expenses have been reduced for the past three months by 25% of previous levels.

2. For every dollar previously spent in telephone expenses, seventy-five cents was expended during the last three months.

The second expression paints a more graphic picture and enables the reviewer to visualize the savings. It's a much stronger way to communicate the real significance of the statistic.

To select the best format, consider the person receiving information from you. A report that is strictly for accounting uses may consist of a column of numbers, perhaps backed up by proof and method of calculation. For top management, a more summarized version may be called for. As we saw in Chapter 1, you may need to revise your material to express it in different ways for different groups.

Let's see how one grouping of information can be written up in different formats. First, a purely numerical expression.

	Expenses
Jan–Mar	$18,000
Apr–Jun	14,630
Jul–Sep	21,342
Oct–Dec	17,650
Total	$71,622

Or you could expand the numerical report with a narrative analysis.

Total expenses for the year were $71,622, broken down as:

1st quarter: 25.1%
2nd quarter: 20.4
3rd quarter: 29.8
4th quarter: 24.7

This represents a reduction of 12% over past year levels, the result of cost-control measures put into effect during the first quarter.

For management, a narrative summary might be best.

Cost-control efforts reduced general expense levels in the division by 12% from the previous year.
We expect the current level to remain in effect as long as controls are enforced.

CHANGING EXPRESSIONS

As you can see from these examples, mathematical fact does not have to be expressed in strictly numerical terms. In fact, there's a psychological aspect to keep in mind: The more you have in a report in the way of numbers, the less significant they become to the reader. You can highlight key points by stating them narratively. You can also make your reports more pertinent by expressing the information in the most applicable form. That's where conversion skills are best used.

To achieve this conversion successfully, begin by visualizing values in their various forms. Many people find it helpful to visualize fractions as parts of a circle. One-half, one-third, and one-fourth are easily comprehended with a picture for reference, even if it is only in our mind's eye. Once we can visualize a value, it is easier to express that value to others.

Think of decimals in terms of dollars and cents. If 1 equals $1, then .35 equals 35 cents; and 4.373 is the same as $4.37 1/3. The same visualizing technique works for percentages. Think of 100% as $1, and relate other percentages to that. This gives you a relative value and helps you concretely see the difference.

Fractions to Decimals

You are likely to come upon a situation in which you need to convert a fractional value to a decimal equivalent.

Example: A supplier writes to you, advising that only 2/7 of your total order can be shipped immediately, with the balance backordered. If the total order was for 1,750 parts, how much will be shipped?

The easiest way to reason out this problem is to put all your information down in fractional form. To make a fraction out of 1,750, put it over a denominator of 1; its value remains unchanged:

$$\frac{2}{7} \times \frac{1,750}{1}$$

Next, multiply each side of the fraction:

$$2 \times 1,750 = 3,500$$

$$7 \times 1 = 7$$

Finally, reduce the fraction 3,500/7 to a whole value, by dividing the top side by the bottom side:

$$3,500 \div 7 = 500$$

Once you have mastered this technique, you can compute the answers without conversion:

$$2 \times 1,750 = 3,500$$

$$3,500 \div 7 = 500$$

If you have trouble visualizing the problem of multiplying by fractions, use the technique of seeing the whole as a pie. In the example above, 2/7 of that pie is available to you. The complete, or whole, value is the number 3,500. Once you can see this in your mind, you can more easily understand and retain the need to multiply.

For the purpose of expressing values in reports, or to speed up the process of calculation, it is often desirable to first convert a fractional value to decimals and then calculate. Decimals are the easiest form for further calculations.

To convert the fraction 2/7 to its decimal equivalent, divide the upper part (the numerator) by the lower part (the denominator).

$$2 \div 7 = .2857$$

$$.2857 \times 1,750 = 500 \text{ parts}$$

A fraction is sometimes included as part of a whole number. In that case, the calculation is more involved than simply converting the fraction.

Example: Your marketing department reports that on average, it takes 7 3/8 sales calls to close one sale in a particular region; the average sale is for $1,133. You are asked to calculate how much the average salesperson grosses for the company on each call. Marketing will use your numbers to set goals for the number of calls that should be made each week in order to meet the sales quota.

Since you know the size of the average sale, and you know that it takes 7 3/8 calls to close a sale, the solution is to divide.

$$\$1,133 \div 7 \ 3/8$$

To make this task easier, convert 7 3/8 to decimal form. Do this by first converting the fractional part, and then adding the whole number 7 to the answer.

$$3 \div 8 = .375$$

$$7 + .375 = 7.375$$

The decimal equivalent of the fraction 7 3/8 is 7.375. Now divide the average sale by the number of calls—expressed in decimal form—to get the answer.

$$\$1,133 \div 7.375 = \$153.63$$

You can now conclude in your report that on average, a salesperson can expect to earn $153.63 each time he or she calls on a customer. To verify this conclusion, reverse it and multiply:

$$\$153.63 \times 7.375 = \$1,133$$

Fractions to Percents

To convert a fraction to a percentage, first convert to a decimal—using the same steps—then shift the decimal point two places to the right. In effect, you are multiplying by 100.

Example: Your shipping department reports that 8/9 of all orders received before 4:00 P.M. are sent out the same day. What percentage does this represent? First convert the fraction to a decimal.

$$8 \div 9 = .8889$$

Then multiply by 100 to find the percentage:

$$.8889 \times 100 = 88.89\%$$

Another form of conversion is reducing a fraction to a lower, more manageable denominator. For example, 1/2 is easier to comprehend than 500/1000.

Decimals to Fractions

To change a decimal statement to a fraction, treat the decimal value as the numerator and use 100 as the denominator.

Decimal Value		Fraction		Reduced Fraction
.31	=	31/100	=	31/100
.18	=	18/100	=	9/50
.50	=	50/100	=	1/2

Decimals to Percentages

Converting a decimal value to a percentage form is blissfully simple: Multiply by 100.

$$.57 \times 100 = 57\%$$
$$.173 \times 100 = 17.3\%$$

Example: You are drafting a report of sales by region for the first quarter. Total sales were $725,423, with the following breakdown:

Eastern region	$263,874
Central region	281,004
Western region	180,545

First calculate the decimals: Divide each of the regional sales by the total, rounding to two decimal places. Then multiply by 100.

$$\$263,874 \div \$725,423 = .36 \times 100 = 36\%$$
$$\$281,004 \div \$725,423 = .39 \times 100 = 39\%$$
$$\$180,545 \div \$725,423 = .25 \times 100 = 25\%$$

Now you can prepare a concise summary statement:

Of total sales, the eastern division accounted for 36%, the central division for 39%, and the western division for 25%.

Percentages to Fractions

Percentage expressions are the most commonly used in business. You may receive information expressed in percentage form, but more readily communicate it as fractions.

Example: You are preparing a narrative report on conditions in your storage warehouse, and want to explain your conclusions using fractions. The following percentages are given to you:

76.3% of all losses occurred on the night shift.
80% of losses were parts worth less than $2.
49.4% of all company losses are due to inventory theft.

When you must report on several factors, fractions often paint a more vivid picture than percentages. To convert from percentages, treat the percentages as the numerator of the fraction, and use 100 as the denominator.

$$76.3\% = 76.3/100$$
$$80\% = 80/100$$
$$49.4\% = 49.4/100$$

Reduce the additional place values in one of two ways: (1) round the value to the nearest whole percentage.

$$76.3\% \text{ rounded} = 76\%$$

Or (2) you can leave the entire value intact and create a larger fraction.

$$76.3\% = 763/1,000$$

The size of the fraction will depend on the number of digits.

$$76.33 = 7,633/10,000$$
$$76.333 = 76,333/100,000$$

Which way should you proceed? Determine how much detail you want to include in your report. In this example, it is safe to assume that 76/100 is much more practical than 7,633/10,000.

To best express your message using fractions, you should first round out the fraction and then express it in its lowest approximate value. All three of the fractions given above can be reduced:

$$76/100 = \text{approximately } 3/4$$
$$80/100 = 4/5$$
$$49/100 = \text{approximately } 1/2$$

Now the statements you include in your report can carry greater weight because of the way you express the information. Compare the two statements below, the first using percentages and the second using fractions.

> Of all inventory losses, 76.3% occur during the night shift. Approximately 80% of loss occurrences are of parts valued at $2 or less. And 49.4% of all company losses are due to theft of inventory.

> Three of every four inventory thefts occur during the night shift. Approximately four-fifths of loss occurrences are of parts worth less than $2. And half of all company losses are due to theft of inventory.

If you communicate your information with reduced fractions, the reader can easily visualize the significance of what you are explaining. "Three of every four" has more impact than "76.3%."

When the percentage is greater than 100, consider the first digit as a whole number and convert only the excess, the portion below 100.

Example: Sales this year are reported to be 225% greater than during the previous year. You want to explain this growth in fractional form. The conversion is a three-step process.

1. Separate the whole number and the fractional part.

$$225\% = 2.25 = 2 + 25/100$$

2. Reduce the fraction.

$$25/100 = 1/4$$

3. Add the whole number and the fraction.

$$2 + 1/4 = 2\,1/4$$

Now you can communicate information in the way you prefer. Using the percentage, your statement might read:

> Sales increased by 225% over the prior year.

A fractional expression may add impact:

Sales increased 2 1/4 times over last year's level.

Percents to Decimals

Converting percentages to decimal form requires only adding a decimal point.

$$49\% = .49$$

Or, if the percentage already contains a decimal, shift it two places to the left.

$$49.3\% = .493$$

Another way to think of it is that you are dividing the percentage value by 100 (the opposite of the procedure for converting a decimal value to a percentage).

Example: Total administrative expenses are to be assigned to various departments on the basis of square footage in the corporate office. You have 14 categories of expense to break down. Three departments have the following portions of the total space.

Accounting	13.5%
Data processing	19.6%
Personnel	9.8%

It's hard to multiply 13.5% by 14; you'll find it much easier if you convert these percentages to decimal form. Move the decimal point two places to the left:

$$13.5\% = .135$$
$$19.6\% = .196$$
$$9.8\% = .098$$

You achieve the same results by dividing the percentage value by 100:

$$13.5 \div 100 = .135$$
$$19.6 \div 100 = .196$$
$$9.8 \div 100 = .098$$

Now that you understand the process for converting from one format to another, here's a shortcut. The accompanying conversion table shows the fractions, percentages, and decimals for the most common values. To work with a value not shown, you'll need to multiply. For instance, if you encounter 5/6:

$$1/6 = .1667$$
$$5/6 = .8335 \ (.1667 \times 5)$$

Conversion Table

Fraction	Percentage	Decimal
1/2	50	.5
1/3	33.33	.3333
1/4	25	.25
1/5	20	.20
1/6	16.67	.1667
1/7	14.29	.1429
1/8	12.5	.125
1/9	11.11	.1111
1/10	10	.1
1/11	9.09	.0909
1/12	8.33	.0833
1/13	7.69	.0769
1/14	7.14	.0714
1/15	6.67	.0667

APPLICATIONS

Practical applications of these conversion techniques will come up frequently in business situations. Some examples:

▪ You are told that 3/8 of sales revenues are derived from the eastern region. How much does that region contribute to the company? To apply this information to total revenues of $18.9 million, you must be able to multiply. First convert the fraction to decimal form, and then multiply:

$$3 \div 8 = .375$$
$$.375 \times \$18.9 = \$7.0875 \text{ million}$$

▪ Delivery expenses are $2,483 in one month. Of that total, 14.38% are to be assigned to the marketing department. What's the dollar value of marketing's deliveries? First convert the percentage to decimal form, then multiply.

$$14.38\% = .1438$$
$$.1438 \times \$2,483 = \$357.06$$

▪ You are asked to report one region's sales as a fraction of total sales last year. Total sales were $16.4 million, and the region's share was $2.05 million.

$$\$2.05 \div \$16.4 = .125$$
$$.125 = 125/1,000$$
$$125/1,000 = 1/8$$

The reduced fractional form is 1/8 [1000 ÷ 125 = 8].

WORK PROJECT

1. Convert the following fractions to decimal form.

1/19   . . . .
3/16   . . . .
18/35   . . . .

2. Convert these decimals to fractions and reduce to their lowest possible form:

.25   . . . .
.68   . . . .
.555   . . . .

3. Write a narrative (that is, non-numerical) version for the following statements.

   a. Total telephone expense, $14,800; estimated personal calls,
      25%.

_____

_____

_____

_____

   b. Monthly revenues $12.8 million; eastern division, approximately
      $3.2 million.

_____

_____

_____

_____

   c. Last month's profit was 8%; this month's 10%.

_____

_____

_____

_____

3
Computing Averages

"The study of mathematics is apt to commence in disappointment . . . like the ghost of Hamlet's father, this great science eludes the efforts of our mental weapons to grasp it."

—Alfred North Whitehead (*An Introduction to Mathematics*, 1911)

An employee of a life insurance company was asked to explain to an independent auditing firm how death benefit reserves had been calculated. He wrote, "Reserves are set up as estimates of the present value of future death claims. Calculations are based on the premise that everyone will eventually die, on average."

Averages are widely used in business communication, and have been a standard method of expressing values: average revenues per salesperson, average overhead cost per division, average production output per worker, average number of sick days per employee.

The mechanics of calculating an average are simple. The trick comes in the logic—in isolating the truly significant information, and presenting it in a way that highlights that significance. Often that means comparing an average to something else; an average by itself seldom has any real value.

Also, guard against overuse. Averages are a popular way to communicate information, because they are simple and quickly grasped. But if you have too many, information loses its real significance.

One other caution: There is a tendency, especially in financial documents, to report information with the use of averages that sound quite positive, even when the news is bad. Few readers are deceived by this tactic. Averages should clarify information, not confuse. The report that minimizes bad news or makes it sound like good news is misleading. A report should convey information accurately, so that appropriate action can be taken.

THE COMPUTATIONS

Averages

To average two or more numbers, add them together and divide the total by the number of factors. So the average of 11, 32, and 80 is 41:

$$11 + 32 + 80 = 123$$
$$123 \div 3 = 41$$

If you add together 4 factors, the sum must be divided by 4 to find the average; and if there are 19, you must divide the sum by 19.

Example: Total sales for one month are $523,950 and your sales force consists of 56 people. How much did the average salesperson sell?

$$\$523,950 \div 56 = \$9,356.25$$

Percentage of Change

In reporting results and trends, it is often necessary to break down an average in comparative form, using both averages and percentages. The computation requires an average and the percentage increase or decrease; see "Percentage Increase" for the procedure.

Example: You must report on the average increase in expenses and the percentage of increase over a prior period.

Month	Expense
Jan	$47,850
Feb	49,201
Mar	54,063

percentage increase

$$\frac{\text{current factor} - \text{prior factor}}{\text{prior factor}}$$

$$\frac{A - B}{B} = \text{percentage increase}$$

First, find the average:

$$47,850 + 49,201 + 54,063 = 151,114$$
$$151,114 \div 3 = 50,371$$

Then compute the percentage increase, first for March over February:

$$\$54,063 - \$49,201 = \$4,862$$
$$\$4,862 \div \$49,201 = 9.9\%$$

Then for February over January:

$$\$49,201 - \$47,850 = \$1,351$$
$$\$1,351 \div \$47,850 = 2.8\%$$

Now you can write your conclusion:

Average expenses for the first quarter were $50,371. However, the expense level increased 9.9% in March and 2.8% during February.

Weighted Averages

When all the factors in your field are of equivalent worth, finding the average is relatively simple: add them together and divide by the number of factors. But when the numbers have different relative worths, you must compute what is called a weighted average.

Example: Your company has two loans outstanding. The first is for $48,000 with an interest rate of 12.625%; the second is for $18,000 with an interest rate of 7.25%. What is the true average interest rate?

If both loans were for the same amount, the procedure would call for adding together the two rates, and then dividing by 2: (12.625 + 7.25) ÷ 2 = 9.9375. But because the principal amounts are different, that is not an accurate answer. The loan carrying the higher interest rate has a greater balance, so the average must be weighted toward that higher rate.

In this example, the total debt of $66,000 consists of:

$$48/66 \text{ at } 12.625\%$$
$$18/66 \text{ at } 7.25\%$$

To find the average, you must multiply each portion by its rate (or "weight") and then add the sums together. See the "Weighted Average" box for a graphic summary of the procedure.

$$(48/66 \times 12.625\%) + (18/66 \times 7.25\%)$$

To make the calculation easier, convert both the fraction and the percents to a decimal equivalent:

$$(.72727 \times .12625) + (.27273 \times .0725)$$

To determine the weighted average, multiply each side of the equation:

$$.72727 \times .12625 = .091818 = 9.1818\%$$
$$.27273 \times .0725 = .019773 = 1.9773\%$$

And then add:

$$9.1818\% + 1.9773\% = 11.16\%$$

weighted average

sum of: **fractional totals**

$$\frac{\text{x rate}}{}$$

= **weighted average**

(A/100 x rate) + (B/100 x rate)

The same weighted average formula can be applied in many business situations. However, often you have to restate information on a like basis before applying the formula.

Example: Your company invests money in securities and earns these profits. What rate of return are you earning?

Amount Invested	Number of Months Held	Amount of Profit
$ 20,000	7	$ 1,450
10,000	14	1,420
10,000	6	385
100,000	22	18,355
40,000	9	3,200
Total $180,000		$24,810

At first glance, it appears the company earned 13.8% ($24,810 divided by $180,000). But investments were held for varying periods, some less than a full year; and different amounts were invested. So that is not an accurate rate of annual average return.

Computing the right answer involves three steps. First, the individual rates must be computed; then they must be expressed on an annualized basis; and finally, the weighted average is computed. (Also see "Annual Rates of Return.")

Step 1: Compute the individual rates. This is done by dividing the amount of profit by the amount of the investment:

$$\$1,450 \div \$20,000 = 7.25\%$$
$$1,420 \div 10,000 = 14.20$$
$$385 \div 10,000 = 3.85$$
$$18,355 \div 100,000 = 18.36$$
$$3,200 \div 40,000 = 8.00$$

Step 2: Express the rates of return on an annualized basis. Divide the percentage of return by the number of months held, and then multiply by 12.

$$(7.25\% \div 7) \times 12 = 12.43\%$$
$$(14.2\% \div 14) \times 12 = 12.17\%$$
$$(3.85\% \div 6) \times 12 = 7.70\%$$
$$(18.36\% \div 22) \times 12 = 10.01\%$$
$$(8.0\% \div 9) \times 12 = 10.67\%$$

Step 3: Compute the weighted average. A total of $180,000 was invested. Express this in fractional form, multiply by the annualized rates of return from step 2, then add the totals.

$$(20/180 \times 12.43\%) + (10/180 \times 12.17\%) + (10/180 \times 7.70\%)$$
$$+ (100/180 \times 10.01\%) + (40/180 \times 10.67\%)$$

This equation can be reduced to:

$$1.38 + 0.68 + 0.43 + 5.56 + 2.37 = 10.42\%$$

This weighted annual return is accurate because it adjusts total returns to an annual basis; and because the return was broken down into fractional parts for the entire amount invested, with the $180,000 total segmented into consistent relative values.

---

annualized rate of return

$$\frac{\text{total return}}{\text{number of months}} \times 12$$

Annual Rates of Return

To find the annualized rate, divide the total return by the amount of months, then multiply by 12 (see "Annualized Rate of Return").

Example: What is the annualized rate of return when you earn 3% in 5 months?

$$(3 \div 5) \times 12 = 7.2\%$$

To find the rate of return for less than one year, divide the annual rate by 12, and multiply by the number of months (see "Part-Year Rate of Return").

Example: The annual rate is 7.2%. What rate of return will you receive in 5 months?

$$(7.2\% \div 12) \times 5 = 3\%$$

The factors in the two tables below are a shortcut for these calculations. Use the first table to find the annualized rate for periods other than one full year. For example, you earn 7% interest over a period of 11 months. The annualized rate of return is 7.637% (7% × 1.091)

Annualized Rate Factors

Months	Factor	Months	Factor	Months	Factor
1	12.000	13	0.923	25	0.480
2	6.000	14	0.857	26	0.462
3	4.000	15	0.800	27	0.444

part–year rate of return

$$\frac{\text{annual rate}}{12} \times \text{number of months}$$

4	3.000	16	0.750	28	0.429
5	2.400	17	0.706	29	0.414
6	2.000	18	0.667	30	0.400
7	1.714	19	0.632	31	0.387
8	1.500	20	0.600	32	0.375
9	1.333	21	0.571	33	0.364
10	1.200	22	0.545	34	0.353
11	1.091	23	0.522	35	0.343
12	1.000	24	0.500	36	0.333

Use the second table to compute monthly rates for annual returns. For example, your annual rate is 8%. The rate for 4 months is 2.664% (8% × 0.333).

Monthly Rate Factors

Months	Factor	Months	Factor	Months	Factor
1	0.083	13	1.083	25	2.083
2	0.167	14	1.167	26	2.167
3	0.250	15	1.250	27	2.250
4	0.333	16	1.333	28	2.333
5	0.417	17	1.417	29	2.417
6	0.500	18	1.500	30	2.500
7	0.583	19	1.583	31	2.583
8	0.667	20	1.667	32	2.667
9	0.750	21	1.750	33	2.750
10	0.833	22	1.833	34	2.833
11	0.917	23	1.917	35	2.917
12	1.000	24	2.000	36	3.000

EFFECTIVE USE OF AVERAGING

The purpose of averages is to make information vivid and visual, whether presented in a report or used to spot and control trends in your company. Say you are preparing a report on the success of expense controls. One way to express it is on the average—per employee, per month, or per dollar of income. For another example, if you compare average sales per person over a period of time, you will see the results of a change in sales management, advertising, or pricing.

Learning how to use averages effectively will make your reporting skills stronger. The key is knowing how to interpret information. Reporting is basically an interpretive skill. To arrange and communicate information, you must first understand what is important. By themselves, averages tell you very little. But next to relevant information from the past, in a budget, or in another division, they become effective control and communication devices.

Example: You prepare a monthly sales report, in which the results from three divisions are averaged. Last month, sales figures were:

Division 1	$34,511.80
Division 2	$46,770.31
Division 3	$21,900.16

Adding up the total ($103,182.27) and dividing by 3, you get an average of $34,394.09.

The next question is, how should this information be reported? The mere average is, by itself, not very significant. To make your report meaningful to others, you must present the averages so that the reader gains some benefit. You could:

1. Report the increase or decrease in average divisional sales over last month.
2. Break down the averages by individual salesperson and report in comparison to prior periods or a forecast level.
3. Compare average divisional sales to average divisional marketing expenditures.

Any of these three presents an average that is more than a mere number. From these types of comparisons, management will be able to judge the relative effectiveness of a division's field management, its own forecasting accuracy, and the success of its promotional efforts.

The Power of Comparisons

As we saw in the last example, merely reporting the "average cost" or the "average production" factor is meaningless. But when one average is compared with another, it takes on a significance, and the information now has life. To see how averages can be effective in reports, review how these three examples read when presented by themselves, and then in comparative form:

> Northfield office reports an average 5 1/2 hours of billable time per 8-hour day, or 41 minutes per hour.
> Northfield office reports 5 1/2 hours of billable time per 8-hour day, compared with 6 3/4 per average employee in the South City office. The productivity factor in South City is 84.4%, compared to a rate in Northfield of only 68.8%.

> Average sales per representative for the last three months are $11,450.
> The average sales representative has reported gross sales of $11,450 per month since the inception of the company's new advertising and direct mail campaign. This compares with a previous average of $9,913, or an overall improvement of 15.5%.

> Telephone expenses per month in the corporate headquarters were $4,706, or an average of $54.72 per person.
> Telephone expense in corporate headquarters now averages $54.72 per person. Six months ago, that average was $71.86. This represents a 24% savings to the company.

Highlight Significant Information

When working with a large number of details, be especially aware of the significance factor. One pitfall of reporting numbers is to wander from what is truly important, and to report too much or the wrong information. Be aware of information and its significance, avoiding these common mistakes:

1. Including more details than are needed for relevant conclusions.
2. Misinterpreting information so that the report lacks meaning to the person receiving it.
3. Reporting in such a way that a conclusion cannot be drawn without asking more questions.

Example: Your company now leases three photocopying machines; management is considering buying the equipment. You are asked to track usage and expenses and report your findings. Increases in usage over the past month have been:

Department	Employees	Prior Month	Current Month
Marketing	12	940	1,402
Accounting	4	385	401
Purchasing	2	66	53
Total	18	1,391	1,856

One way to report this increase is:

> Average photocopy use per employee increased from 77 last month to 103 this month. Most of that increase occurred in the marketing department, which was responsible for 99.4% of the total increase (117 copies per employee compared to 78 in the previous month).

This identifies the source of the increase, but does not explain what is truly significant. The report could go on to identify the cause of the increase:

> This increased usage is due to the distribution of the department's quarterly sales report to all field offices, and is expected to recur on a quarterly basis.

But this still does not help the person reading the report to *understand* the important point about the month-to-month change in expense. Another way to report this information is on a relative cost basis (you'll need to gather some additional data).

Photocopying expenses for the month were $0.87 per copy, compared to $1.08 last month.

	June	July
Machine rental	$1,135	$1,135
Supplies	230	301
Copies (.10 each)	139	186
Total	$1,504	$1,622
Average cost per copy	$1.08	$0.87

Which is more significant? The first report identifies where usage occurs, and then explains why costs rose. But the second report shows that with a portion of the costs fixed, increased volume results in a lower unit cost. The second version contains conclusive information: Unit cost declines with usage.

It means little to identify the relative percentage of use by department. Perhaps the average use per employee has some significance if it implies excessive personal use of the equipment. So a trend over time is often useful and significant. In the example above, the cost per unit is relevant if you are trying to prove the cost-effectiveness of leasing a photocopy machine.

To interpret what is significant, you must understand the purpose behind the analysis. This exercise proves that the cost of leasing is lower per unit when usage increases. So relative efficiency of the machine must be compared to current and estimated future use. If a comparable machine is purchased rather than leased, the comparison should include physical depreciation and the cost of maintenance, rather than a set monthly lease expense.

Apply logic to every factual report, making sure your conclusions are meaningful *and* useful. A report like this should address key questions:

1. How does the information help to reduce costs in the future? Or, in this case, how does the information justify carrying a particular expense on the books?
2. How can the results be reported so that future expense controls and budgeting can be improved?
3. What significant trends should be identified and, if necessary, corrected?

Provide for Relevant Conclusions

All too often, business reports either are inconclusive or draw conclusions unrelated to the facts. For example:

- You may follow a trend in average gross sales and ignore the fact that the percentage of net profits is declining.
- The average units of production per shift are on the rise, but the ratio of defects is rising even faster, so the net result is a higher unit cost.
- The average growth in the level of an expense seems reasonable compared to sales. However, the expense is actually excessively high, and is not being controlled.

Averages can also be deceiving if they are not interpreted correctly, or if they are used in ways that do not accurately report a significant trend.

Example: The following results have been reported for the first quarter:

Month	Total Sales	Number of Employees	Office Supplies
Jan	$134,600	82	$3,150
Feb	155,833	82	3,414
Mar	158,660	81	3,545

How should office expense trends be reported in this situation? Compare the three conclusions below:

1. Sales for the first quarter increased by 17.9% per month, from $134,600 to $158,660. During the same period, office supply expense levels rose by only 12.5%.

2. Average sales for the period were $149,698 while average monthly office supply expenses were $3,370 (2.3% of sales).

3. Average monthly office supply expenses per employee for the first quarter were $38 (January); $42 (February); and $44 (March).

The third report is the most meaningful. The level of office supplies is more related to the average use per employee than to trends in sales.

When results are reported in such a way that no useful conclusions can be drawn, they are of no value. With the first two reports, what actions can management take to reduce office expenses? In the first case, the rise in office expenses is less than the rise in sales. This could be interpreted as a positive trend, when in fact there is no relationship whatsoever. In the second, no trend is reported; facts are merely arranged. A significant conclusion can be drawn from the third case: "Office expenses per employee rose each month during the first quarter." Management now has the information it needs to take corrective action.

WORK PROJECT

1. You have two loans outstanding: one for $32,000 at 11.25%, the second for $82,000 at 6%. What is the true average interest rate? Hint: Use the weighted average formula. ....

2. Sales were $82,380 in October, $78,318 in September, and $72,450 in August. Compute the following:

a. Average sales for the period.   ....
b. Percentage increase for
    October over September   ....
    September over August   ....
    October over August   ....
    October over the average ....

3. Compute the annualized rate of return for the following total returns:

a. 12% in 15 months.   ....
b. 14% in 22 months.   ....
c. 6% in 11 months.   ....

4. Compute the part-year rates of return for the following annual rates:

   a. 9% for 7 months.   ....
   b. 12% for 5 months.   ....
   c. 14% for 3 months.   ....

4

Interpreting Ratios

" 'So so' is good, very good, very excellent good; and yet it is not; it is but so so."

—William Shakespeare, *As You Like It*

An accounting manager was having difficulty explaining to one employee how to compute ratios. Finally, realizing the employee was a horse racing fan, he compared ratio analysis to the track. "Now do you understand what I mean by saying the current ratio is two to one at the end of the second quarter?" he asked. The employee answered, "Yes. Assets were favored two to one in the second, and finished ahead by a full length."

Communicating business information depends on comparisons. The only way to effectively judge whether a report is positive or negative is to look at it next to something else: the results from a previous period, another division, or a universally accepted standard.

For example, how do you describe last year's sales, production, or marketing results? Were they so-so? Good? Excellent? And, more to the point, on what basis do you make that judgment? To report that "results are good" or "performance is so-so" tells nothing; the information has to be placed on a scale, put next to a well-accepted and well-understood measure of results, before it takes on significance.

In the last chapter, averages were shown to be a valuable tool in this process. Another way to express comparisons is with the use of ratios.

47

Ratios summarize comparisons and, at the same time, breathe life into numbers.

Example: A new supervisor has been appointed to the customer service department. Six months later, management wants to know whether the change has resulted in higher productivity, lower cost, and better overall performance.

You may report, "The new supervisor is working out well." This is an opinion, not a supportable fact. By what standard has the supervisor been measured? How can you prove that putting him in charge was a good move? There are several ways to evaluate the situation, but in order to report on productivity, which is what management asked for, you must use an analysis of some type. You could support your conclusion with:

1. Time required to respond to customer complaints, compared to response time six months ago.
2. Level of recurring complaints.
3. Cost information (broken down on a per-complaint basis, for example).

Using ratios in this situation will help clarify your report. Let's see how reports of the three analyses might look, first without and then with use of ratios. First, reporting on the time required to respond to complaints.

> The average complaint required 1.3 days for resolution. During the prior period, this average was 2.8 days.

> The time required for resolution of customer complaints has improved 215% during the last six months.

Reporting on the basis of recurring complaints:

> Six months ago there were an average of 134 complaints per month unresolved after the first inquiry. During the current six months, that average dropped to 51.

> Response to first calls from customers improved during the most recent six-month period by the rate of 2.6 to 1.

Reporting cost information:

> Monthly expenses for the customer service department averaged $38.15 per complaint in the previous six-month period, and $29.80 in the most recent six months.

> Monthly expenses per complaint in the customer service department were 1.28 times more efficient during the last six months than during the previous six months.

WORKING WITH RATIOS

You may have noticed that in the examples above, the ratios were expressed differently. A ratio can be given in any of three forms, depending upon the type of information being reported:

1. The percentage form.
2. The x to y form (when x is the current value and y is the previous value).
3. The number of times an event occurred.

All three forms are different expressions of the same information. See "Ratio Expressions" for a quick summary.

The Computations

A ratio, remember, is a way to express change over time—how one factor changed in comparison to another factor. Calculating the ratio requires division: divide the previous number by the present one.

Example: After six months, unresolved customer complaints dropped from an average of 134 per month to 51. How would you express that as a ratio? First, calculate the change factor by dividing.

$$134 \div 51 = 2.63$$

ratio expressions

1. PERCENTAGE

occurrence of defects improved
from 1 in 12 to 1 in 27   =   225%

2. X TO Y

6,402 units compared with 5,812   =   1.1 to 1

3. NUMBER OF TIMES

improvement in cost per unit
from $1.96 to $1.44   =   1.36 times

This can be put into ratio form in three ways:

263% improvement
2.6-to-1 better response
2.6 times more responsive

Take another look at "Ratio Expressions." All three formats are calculated by dividing the later number into the earlier one.

Be careful in computing a ratio expression that involves fractional values. For example, when last period's defects were 1 in 12, and this period's were 1 in 27, the improvement is 225%:

$$27 \div 12 = 2.25, \text{ or } 225\%$$

Evaluate Results: Positive and Negative

To develop ratios in reports, it is first necessary to understand whether a comparative result is positive or negative. It will affect how you do your computations.

Are the results positive or negative? Common sense will guide you. When comparing units produced from one period to another, it is assumed that higher productivity is desirable. Thus, a greater number of units in the latest period is positive information. A lower cost per unit is also assumed to be positive; so is a decrease in defects, even though they are smaller numbers.

Once you have that clearly in mind, use this guide to computing ratios:

- A favorable (positive) *increase* (numbers of units or dollars, for example) is converted to ratio form by dividing the later factor by the earlier one.

Example: Sales were $425,800 for the latest quarter, compared with $388,734 previously. First, divide the later factor by the earlier:

$$\$425,800 \div \$388,734 = 1.095$$

Then convert to the desired ratio form:

Percentage	109.5%
x to *y*	1.1 to 1
Number of times	1.1 times higher

- A favorable (positive) *decrease* (cost per unit, for example) can be converted to ratio form in the same manner, but the resulting ratio will be less than 100%.

Example: Your cost per unit produced this period was $12.83, compared with $15.80 last period. First, divide the later factor by the earlier:

$$\$12.83 \div \$15.80 = .81$$

Then convert to the desired ratio form:

Percentage	81%
x to y	0.81 to 1
Number of times	.81 times lower

You can also express this in reverse form. Divide the *earlier* factor by the *later:*

$$\$15.80 \div \$12.83 = 1.23$$

Convert to the desired ratio form:

Percentage	123% higher (in the previous period)
x to y	1.2 to 1 (in the previous period)
Number of times	1.2 times greater (previous period)

Choose the Best Format

When is one form used over another? For financial ratios that are reported every time a statement is prepared on the same format, specific expressions are used consistently (more on this later in the chapter). But for reporting information like the customer-service example, any of the three forms is acceptable. The key is to use the one that best expresses the significance of a change.

You may use a mix of all three forms to present a lot of information when using just one would make your report sound redundant. You may be called on to summarize a number of similar results, when it is desirable to avoid merely listing a column of numbers. In this case, varying your report with ratios can help change the tempo of your narrative.

Example: You are summarizing the following information:

| | Units of Production | | |
Division	2nd Qtr.	1st Qtr.	Change
Northeast	140,610	121,400	15.8%
East	99,050	88,420	12.0
Southeast	136,735	154,600	(13.1)
South	101,800	100,342	1.5
Midwest	47,650	55,900	(17.3)
Pacific	108,593	107,845	0.7
International	66,002	74,035	(12.2)
Total	700,440	702,542	(0.3%)

This format itself—a listing of numbers—will do for a strictly accounting report. But to summarize the information in a narrative report, you are faced with the task of segmenting the information into a more visual and interesting form.

Don't produce a narrative that merely repeats the numbers.

Total production for the second quarter was less than production for the first quarter, broken down as follows: increases in the Northeast (15.8%), East (12.0%), South (1.5%), and Pacific (0.7%) divisions; and decreases in the Southeast (13.1%), Midwest (17.3%), and International (12.2%) divisions.

Do work in some variation:

An overall reduction of 0.3% in production during the second quarter consists of significant increases in two regions, offset by significant decreases in three others.

Leading in production increase for the quarter was the Northeast division, which produced 1.15 units for every 1 produced during the previous quarter. The East division also had a substantial increase, experiencing 12% greater production.

Significant decreases were reported in the Midwest, operating at 85% of last quarter's rate; Southeast, which had a 13.1% decline; and International, where only .89 units were produced for each during the previous period.

Small increases were reported in the South and Pacific divisions.

The second version accomplishes two things. First, if you vary the ratio method, the report is easier to read and absorb. Second, it rearranges the sequence of the information, so that the reader can better understand the order of significance.

Effective Presentations

In order for a ratio to be useful as a control tool, it must be valid and you must be able to draw a meaningful conclusion from it. That means the data must be accurate, and the ratio must be presented in context. Faulty ratios lead to flawed conclusions. If a ratio reports the wrong information, no corrective action can be taken.

To convey the true significance, a ratio must compare two related values. It is the change in *relative* status that allows management to put control measures into effect, change a marketing or administrative strategy, or correct a financially weak situation.

For example, a monthly report showing total sales per employee—and nothing else—is meaningless. These raw numbers show no direct relationship between employees and sales, indicate no trends to correct or encourage, and permit no action or control measure. But if a sales manager reports total sales by representative, including their ratio to past totals, this is useful information. It provides incentive to salespeople to meet and exceed those levels. It also shows sales management which salespeople are accounting for the greater portion of sales, and which ones are performing below par.

Ratios should always be presented as the latest update of a trend. (Trend analysis is explained in the next chapter.) Combining the use of averages and ratios and then putting reported data into a context makes information meaningful and useful.

FINANCIAL RATIOS

A company's financial statement gives a picture of its economic well-being. It reports figures for key aspects of the business as of a specific time. You can see more of the picture if you relate two aspects to each other. What you get then is a financial ratio, a way to explain trends and changes in results. Every financial ratio has a distinct purpose and significance. To use them as effective reporting tools, you must first understand them. The most common financial ratios are explained below.

Current Ratio

This is a comparison between current assets and current liabilities. "Current" means one year or less. A current asset is cash or an asset that can be converted to cash within 12 months. A current liability is a debt owed within the next year. If, for example, your statement includes a loan that must be repaid over the next 48 months, the total value of the next 12 payments is current and the rest is long-term.

To calculate this ratio, divide current assets by current liabilities; see "Current Ratio" box. The current ratio is always expressed in x to y format. As a general rule, a ratio of 2 to 1 or higher is considered an indication that the company is managing its cash flow effectively. A ratio below that (with the asset number lower than 2) is a sign of cash-control weakness; the lower the ratio, the more severe the problem.

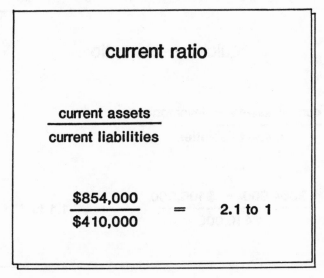

current ratio

$$\frac{\text{current assets}}{\text{current liabilities}}$$

$$\frac{\$854,000}{\$410,000} = 2.1 \text{ to } 1$$

Example: Current assets (consisting of cash, marketable securities, accounts receivable, and inventory) total $243,850. Current liabilities (consisting of accounts and taxes payable and the current portion of notes payable) total $111,900. To compute the ratio, divide current assets by current liabilities:

$$\$243,850 \div \$111,900 = 2.18 \text{ to } 1$$

Example: Current assets total $544,722, and current liabilities are $619,736. The current ratio is unfavorable, as it is lower than 2 to 1:

$$\$544,722 \div \$619,736 = 0.88 \text{ to } 1$$

Quick Assets Ratio

This is similar to the current ratio, except that values of inventory are excluded (see "Quick Assets Ratio" box). As a general rule, a quick assets ratio of 1 to 1 is considered acceptable evidence of good cash flow control. When an analysis compares changes in current *and* quick assets

---

quick assets ratio

$$\frac{\text{current assets} - \text{inventories}}{\text{current liabilities}}$$

$$\frac{\$854,000 - \$406,000}{\$410,000} = 1.1 \text{ to } 1$$

ratios, it is possible to draw conclusions about inventory's relative significance as a factor in controlling cash flow.

Companies that do not keep inventories should use the quick assets ratio, and apply the 1 to 1 standard. Like the current ratio, quick assets are always expressed in the *x* to *y* form.

Example: A company that does not have inventory shows current assets of $201,960 and current liabilities of $210,955. The quick assets ratio is slightly below the acceptable level of 1 to 1:

$$\$201,960 \div \$210,955 = 0.96 \text{ to } 1$$

Example: Current assets (including inventory) are $123,745. Inventory is valued at $42,500. Current liabilities are $74,850. The current ratio is 1.65 to 1, below the acceptable standard of 2 to 1. However, quick assets are within the acceptable range:

$$\frac{\$123,745 - \$42,500}{\$74,850} = 1.09 \text{ to } 1$$

Turnover in Working Capital

This is another ratio concerned with the effective use of available funds. It compares "working capital" to total sales. Working capital is the difference between current assets and current liabilities. If these are approximately equal, or if liabilities exceed assets, there is no working capital.

Turnover refers to the complete replacement of working capital. It's an average only, meant to measure use of capital to generate sales. On average cash, inventory, and accounts receivable "turn" a given number of times during the year. But in fact, you don't replace one level of working capital with another. The turnover average itself moves upward or downward, and the measured comparison is the basis for developing and controlling a trend.

Total sales for the period are divided by working capital as of the close of a period; see "Turnover in Working Capital." For example, if you want to compute turnover in working capital for one year, you must divide the total sales for the total year by the working capital at the *end*

turnover in working capital

$$\frac{\text{net sales}}{\text{current assets} - \text{current liabilities}}$$

$$\frac{\$4{,}835{,}000}{\$854{,}000 - \$410{,}000} = 10.9 \text{ times}$$

of the year. And if the computation is for a quarter, the quarter's sales are divided by the ending working capital.

This ratio measures how effectively a company is able to convert current assets into operating cash. If sales are increasing rapidly, but so is the level of accounts receivable and inventories, the turnover in working capital will slow down. The ratio is expressed in the form of the number of occurrences.

Example: Your company's current assets are $325,800 and current liabilities are $140,640. Total sales for the prior year were $1,835,300. Compute working capital turnover by dividing total sales by the difference in current assets and liabilities:

$$\frac{\$1{,}835{,}300}{\$325{,}800 - \$140{,}640} = 9.9 \text{ times}$$

There is no set standard for measuring whether a turnover ratio is or is not at an acceptable level. It takes on meaning only when compared to last quarter's or last year's ratio. Every company will develop its own definition of acceptability, depending upon volume, capitalization, and the margin of profit.

Inventory Turnover

This ratio measures the number of times the average level of inventory is sold. While every item in stock may not be physically disposed of during a period of time, and obviously no single item will literally be sold more than once, the average level will be sold a given number of times during the year; see "Inventory Turnover" box.

Turnover indicates how efficiently the inventory level is controlled by a company. For example, if the rate of turnover (always expressed in the number of turns) declines over time, it indicates that inventory levels are too high and are not being properly controlled.

One popular way of computing turnover is by comparing average inventories to net sales. However, inventory is listed on the balance sheet at cost, while sales are reported in marked-up form. So the comparison is not on the same basis. If the mix of sales involves products with different percentages of markup, that will distort turnover. The correct comparison is made between average inventory and the cost of goods sold, the actual raw cost of the products.

Example: Average inventory is $120,000 for the prior year. Total sales were $886,400. Turnover is computed on the basis of these totals:

$$\$886,400 \div \$120,000 = 7.4 \text{ times}$$

---

inventory turnover

$$\frac{\text{cost of goods sold}}{\text{average inventory}}$$

$$\frac{\$2,910,000}{\$414,000} = 7.0 \text{ times}$$

However, the company markets two different classes of product. One is marked up 85%, and the other is marked up only 32%. The cost of goods sold will vary widely, depending upon product mix. True costs may range anywhere between $479,135 and $671,515:

$$\$886,400 \div 1.85 = \$479,135$$
$$\$886,400 \div 1.32 = \$671,515$$

So the correct turnover is actually somewhere in between 4.0 and 5.6 times:

$$\$479,135 \div \$120,000 = 4.0 \text{ times}$$
$$\$671,515 \div \$120,000 = 5.6 \text{ times}$$

Make sure you start with an accurate figure for average inventory; the computation is based on volatility in stock levels. If your inventory is about the same value throughout the year, you can compute the average simply by adding beginning and ending balances, and dividing by 2.

Example: Your firm's beginning inventory is $425,800 and ending inventory is $455,000:

$$(\$425,800 + \$455,000) \div 2 = \$440,400$$

The accuracy of this average will vary if inventory levels change drastically throughout the year.

Example: Your company experiences seasonal variances in inventory levels. For the beginning of the year and each of the four quarters, inventory was valued at:

January 1	$107,450
March 31	122,650
June 30	186,200
September 30	245,320
December 31	122,000

In this case, add the beginning balance and each of the quarter-ending balances, and divide by 5:

$$(107,450 + 122,650 + 186,200 + 245,320 + 122,000) \div 5 = \$156,724$$

Once you have computed a fair average, divide it into the cost of goods sold to determine the number of turns.

Example: Your company reports average inventory of $156,724. The cost of goods sold for the same period was $932,400:

$$\$932,400 \div \$156,724 = 5.9 \text{ times}$$

Debt/Equity Ratio

This ratio shows the comparison between two types of capitalization (sources of funds): debt and equity. A company gets its funds either from people who invest in the firm (thereby purchasing a share of its equity) or by borrowing. The higher the portion of the total that is represented by debt, the greater the cost of carrying that debt. Interest must be paid on loans; and larger loans create larger interest obligations. As the ratio of debt increases, the future profits can be expected to decline. For this reason, a company will want to maintain its debt/equity ratio at a reasonable level. What is "reasonable" depends on profitability, future expansion programs and how they are to be funded, and the overall size and earning power of a company. No one rule of thumb can be applied to every company. Judge the debt/equity relationship as part of a trend, over time.

This ratio is expressed in percentage form, and is computed by dividing total liabilities by tangible net worth; see "Debt/Equity Ratio" box. Tangible net worth is the total of all assets less all liabilities, excluding intangible assets (such as goodwill or the assigned value of covenants not to compete and other contractual rights).

Example: A company reports net worth of $843,650. Liabilities are $410,830. Included in the company's assets is an intangible value for goodwill of $50,000. To compute the debt/equity ratio:

$$\frac{\$410,830}{\$843,650 - \$50,000} = 51.8\%$$

To interpret the significance of this ratio: The company's total debt is 51.8% of equity.

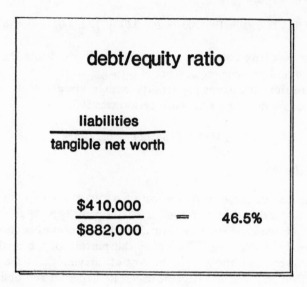

Return on Sales

This popular ratio is the proportion of net sales represented by net profits. It is calculated by dividing sales into profits and reported in precentage form (see "Return on Sales" box). A distinction should be made between pretax and aftertax profits.

You can evaluate return in comparison to other companies in the same industry. Check the record of your publicly listed competitors, or use the standard of the industry as it is understood in your company.

Example: Your company's sales for the year are $1,423,095, and aftertax profits are $74,506. The return on sales is computed by dividing profits by sales:

$$\$74,506 \div \$1,423,095 = 5.2\%$$

Return on Capital

A variation of the return ratio is to compute net profits on the basis of capital in the company, rather than sales; see "Return on Capital" box. For consistency and accuracy, the value of capital should be the amount

return on sales

net profit
―――――
sales

$$\frac{\$322,000}{\$4,835,000} = 6.7\%$$

available at the beginning of the year; and net profits should be the total for the entire period. This makes the ratio valid: The capital at the beginning of the period was applied to produce the reported profits.

Beginning capital must be adjusted for two factors:

1. Reduced for any intangible assets included on the balance sheet.
2. Increased proportionally for any additional capital contributed during the year.

Investors expect returns that are competitive with alternative investments in the same industry. To judge the health of your ratio, use historical information relating to return on capital.

Example: A corporation reports net profits of $110,300 and beginning capital of $1,007,450. However, the balance sheet includes intangible assets of $30,000.

$$\frac{\$110,300}{\$1,007,450 - \$30,000} = 11.3\%$$

Example: A company's profits for the year were $72,600. Beginning capital was $785,000 and another $100,000 was paid in October 1.

The first step is to adjust the equity. The paid-in capital was available for only 3 of the 12 months of the year. So its value in the computation should be adjusted to one-fourth its total:

$$\$100,000 \div 4 = \$25,000$$

The beginning capital is then adjusted to reflect the *average* available capital:

$$\$785,000 + \$25,000 = \$810,000$$

Now compute the ratio.

$$\$72,600 \div \$810,000 = 9.0\%$$

In this example, average available capital during the year produced a 9% return.

Collection Ratio

This is a computation of the time required to collect money due. Accounts receivable must be controlled in order for a company to maintain healthy cash flow. It commonly occurs that sales and profits increase rapidly in a relatively short period of time, but cash flow becomes critical—a sign that collections are not being as rigidly enforced as in the past.

Following the average number of days required to collect money will show a trend in the control of outstanding receivables. This ratio is always expressed in the number of days in the collection period; see "Collection Ratio."

When gathering information, strive for accuracy.

1. Include only sales made on account. Cash sales should be excluded from this analysis.

2. Adjust sales for any extraordinary items, such as one-time single-item sales, or adjustments to sales that will not be repeated.

3. Adjust average accounts receivable for any large bad debts written off during the period, to ensure a consistent and dependable basis for your conclusions.

return on capital

net profit
tangible net worth

$$\frac{\$322,000}{\$882,000} = 36.5\%$$

4. If accounts receivable balances are approximately the same level each month, you can use beginning and ending annual or quarterly balances to compute the average. But if the amount outstanding varies greatly from one month to another, use the beginning balance and the ending balance each month in computing an average.

Example: Your company had total credit sales for the last 12 months of $18,435,750. Accounts receivable were $2,055,600 at the beginning of the year and $2,424,680 at the end of the year. To compute the ratio, first find average accounts receivable (if the balance varies widely during the year, use quarterly or monthly balances rather than beginning and ending balances only):

$$\frac{\$2,055,600 + \$2,424,680}{2} = \$2,240,140$$

Next, divide total sales by the number of days in the year to determine the average daily sale. Use 365, even if your company does not operate on holidays or weekends. Money is outstanding on those nonworking days as well as on business days:

$$\$18,435,750 \div 365 = \$50,509$$

collection ratio

average accounts receivable
---
average daily sales

$$\frac{\$595,400}{\$13,247} = 44.9 \text{ days}$$

Divide average receivables ($2,240,140) by average daily sales ($50,509), and express the collection ratio in the number of days:

$$\$2,240,140 \div \$50,509 = 44.4 \text{ days}$$

WORK PROJECT

1. Your marketing department reports that 62,800 units were sold last year, compared with 51,011 in the previous year. Explain this in all three ratio forms:

    a. Percentage   ....
    b. X to y   ....
    c. Number of times ....

2. The cost of advertising for each dollar in sales during the fourth quarter was 35 cents. During the same quarter last year, it was 22 cents. Explain this change in all three ratio forms:

a. Percentage   . . . .
b. X to y   . . . .
c. Number of times . . . .

3. Net profits were $81,650 last year, and $72,005 the year before. Write three narrative descriptions of this change.

_____

_____

_____

_____

_____

_____

4. A company's latest financial statement reports this information:

Current assets	$ 186,550	
Long-term assets	425,811	
Intangible assets	10,000	
Total		$622,361
Current liabilities	$ 89,307	
Long-term liabilities	145,600	
Total liabilities	$ 234,907	
Net worth	387,454	
Total		$622,361
Total sales	$1,745,800	
Cost of goods sold	1,108,300	
Gross profit	$ 637,500	
Operating expenses	518,800	
Net profit	$ 118,700	

Compute these ratios:

a. Current ratio   . . . .
b. Turnover in working capital   . . . .
c. Debt/equity ratio   . . . .
d. Return on sales   . . . .∴.

5

Trend Analysis

"The move toward profitability has been underscored by the reduction of losses by over 50% as compared to the prior year."

—From the annual report of a corporation with three years' consecutive losses.

The owner of a small management consulting firm applied for a line of credit. Reviewing the latest financial statement, the loan officer commented that profits declined each year for three years, and called it a negative trend. The owner defended his numbers. "Yes, if you look at the three-year trend, it's down. But the one-year trend is excellent."

In the last chapter we saw how ratios can help summarize significant information for management. But as we know, a ratio by itself is meaningless. It can be judged only as part of a series, the latest phase of a trend that has been developing over time. The accumulated strengths and weaknesses in financial status show management the direction the company is moving.

There are three classes of trends:

1. *Positive.* When results are improving over the past—sales and profits are higher, production is more efficient, the financial strength indicated by a ratio is better than last year's—that's a positive trend.

2. *Negative.* These trends point out the need for management action. They are useful only if a solution to the problem can be identified. For

example, when profits are lower while the volume of sales is increasing, there's a problem—and an answer.

3. *Flat.* Some trends show that status is not changing. In a financial sense, the situation is no better and no worse than before. For example, your company's management has stated that on average, accounts receivable should be collected in 45 to 50 days. As long as the trend remains within this boundary, it is acceptable.

START WITH GOOD INFORMATION

Past financial information is the most dependable source for future prediction. In preparing budgets and forecasts, for example, the trend of the past year can be used to estimate next year's level. Past information also helps to control expense levels or to set performance goals, income volumes, or efficiency levels in production. Once management becomes aware of a past level, it is better able to predict and control the future because it knows what actions to take now.

Example: Your company reports a decreasing return on sales for the last four years, while sales volume has been increasing:

	Sales	Profits	Ratio
Four years ago	$4.6 million	$382,000	8.3%
Three years ago	4.9 million	387,000	7.9%
Two years ago	5.8 million	401,000	6.9%
One year ago	6.1 million	403,000	6.6%

Looking at profits alone, you might conclude a positive trend, because the amount of profit has been rising each year. But in fact, the *ratio* of net profits has been on the decline. Information like this provides management a good handle on the problem.

In order for trends to work in your reporting, three factors must be present:

1. The information must be correct. If not, your conclusions will be wrong.

2. The past must be a reliable indicator. If conditions have changed, past information may be invalidated.
3. The interpretation and reporting of data in the form of trends must lead to a conclusion and point the way to solutions.

Example: You are given the assignment of developing a system to control telephone expenses. This will include the design of daily phone logs for long distance calls, reviews and comparisons of billings, and installation of a phone system that will identify usage by station.

In your analysis of past phone expenses, you identify the average monthly phone bill on the basis of total per employee. The trend shows a gradual increase in this level. However, upon further review, you find several factors that will affect the accuracy of your trend.

For one thing, the totals you have been using for phone expense are incorrect. Part of the expense was assigned out to divisions, so the total does not include all expenses. The company has now stopped adjusting telephone expenses. So the latest expense levels appear much higher than earlier ones.

For another, at the beginning of the year the company opened a new international division. Phone expenses assigned to this activity are greater than the average domestic bill. So the comparison from one year to the next is inaccurate.

Also, expansion has led to the addition of more than 200 new employees, primarily in the manufacturing and shipping departments. Most of them do not use telephones routinely, so your per-employee analysis has been thrown off.

The moral of the story is that a trend analysis that uses surface information is not necessarily accurate, and that conclusions drawn may be wrong. In this example, an investigation of the *nature* of expense reveals there is more to the increase than meets the eye.

THREE COMMON MISTAKES

Theories of trend analysis work well. A textbook example showing how to manage information and draw a conclusion has one flaw: Everything you need is provided to you. In the real world, variables and incomplete data are common.

Misinterpretation

Financial information is not necessarily part of a trend. A common trap is misinterpretation of data, drawing one conclusion when the real, meaningful trend shows something entirely different. This usually occurs when averages or ratios are used out of context.

For example, one division of your company used to lead in total sales. But over the last three years, its numbers have been dropping steadily. When results are averaged over a four-year period, this division is still the leader, overall. But reviewing each year's results, you see there is obviously a negative trend.

	Total Sales			
Division	4 Years Ago	3 Years Ago	2 Years Ago	1 Year Ago
Northeast	$835,000	$783,000	$753,000	$701,000
East	640,000	665,000	683,000	710,000
South	351,000	355,000	360,000	358,000
Midwest	166,000	172,000	201,000	187,000
West	427,000	484,000	466,000	475,000

This information could be reported in a misleading way, such as the following summary:

Total Sales, Last Four Years

Division	Total Sales	Yearly Average
Northeast	$3,072,000	$768,000
East	2,698,000	674,500
South	1,424,000	356,000
Midwest	726,000	181,500
West	1,852,000	463,000

The northeast division continues to lead in total sales volume
based on averages over the last four years.

This gives the appearance that the northeast division continues as leader. However, sales have slipped seriously, while other divisional totals have generally been on the rise. A more accurate report would summarize the trend:

Trends in Sales, Last Four Years

Division	Percentage of Total Sales			
	Year 4	Year 3	Year 2	Year 1
Northeast	34.5%	31.8%	30.6%	28.8%
East	26.4	27.1	27.7	29.2
South	14.5	14.4	14.6	14.7
Midwest	6.9	7.0	8.2	7.7
West	17.7	19.7	18.9	19.6

Total sales have remained relatively flat over the past four years. This is due to significant decreases in sales in the northeast division; other divisions reported minor increases in sales volume.

An accurate trend has now been shown. There is a problem in the northeast division. In the first report, management has no indication of this trend, because the reporter misread the trend and unintentionally buried it instead of revealing it.

Now you have the basis for an investigation and suggestions for improvements of the trend. Some possibilities:

1. A change in the regional market or in the level of competition.
2. A decreased number of sales representatives.
3. A change in management.
4. Product or pricing changes.

If you are not in a position to investigate the causes of unfavorable trends (because of either your location or limits on your investigative authority), you can only report the facts and suggest what should be investigated by someone else. It is then management's responsibility to decide what actions should be taken.

Extraneous Data

A trend can be distorted when isolated information is introduced to otherwise valid trend data. For example, net profits one year include a one-time adjustment for a change in inventory valuation method. In order for a trend analysis to remain accurate and useful for predictions, financial results must be adjusted to exclude nonrepetitive information.

Seasonal Changes

A trend can be misrepresentative when seasonal variations are interpreted incorrectly. For example, sales totals for the first six months were:

Month	Sales
January	$123,700
February	118,400
March	128,500
April	129,500
May	142,600
June	168,300

You might conclude from this that sales are on a very positive upward trend, and project the year's total at a level much higher than it will be.

When seasonal factors are at play, you must use the average increases from past years to accurately predict future levels. In the case of seasonally adjusted sales, you may accurately predict monthly levels based on relative ups and downs in the past. If June, July, and August are normally 15 to 20% higher than the *average* month, and have consistently come in at those levels for the last three years, that's a dependable basis for predicting this year's level, even when volumes are much different than in the past.

Memory Jogger: Is It Really a Trend?

Predictions are only as accurate as the information used to develop trends. Watch out for the three common errors made in trend analysis:

1. *Misinterpretation.* Do not arrange information so that the significant changes are not reported, or hidden in the averages. Be sure your reporting discloses what management needs to know in order to improve the future.

2. *Extraneous data.* Adjust financial results that include extraordinary items.

Failure to adjust for one-time income, cost or expense items, and other nonrepetitive information will distort the accuracy of your report.

3. *Seasonal change.* Many trends are vulnerable to misinterpretation because of seasonal changes. Be sure you adjust your report based on historical changes in levels of income, costs, and expenses.

INTERPRETING INFORMATION: TREND ANALYSIS

Once you ensure that your information is relevant, consistent, and correct, you can prepare a trend analysis. To make your reports effective, you must be certain you are interpreting the data correctly. Examples of trend analysis, using the ratios explained in the last chapter, are given here. Each example is accompanied by an illustration and explanation. Trends can also be made visual and understandable with the use of graphs, a technique that will be explained fully in Chapter 6.

Current Ratio Trend

The following results were reported on balance sheets ending each quarter:

Quarter	Current Assets	Current Liabilities
Mar 31	$1,450,900	$823,500
Jun 30	1,862,600	845,000
Sep 30	1,650,400	821,300
Dec 31	1,318,700	798,600

Current ratios (computed by dividing current assets by current liabilities) for each quarter are:

Mar 31	1.76 to 1
Jun 30	2.20 to 1
Sep 30	2.01 to 1
Dec 31	1.65 to 1

The correct interpretation and reporting of this ratio depends largely on what has occurred in the past (see "Analysis of Current Ratio"). If the ratio has been consistently above 2 to 1 in the past, and this variance is below normal, it indicates a problem in cash flow. Similarly, a previously consistent ratio, followed by widely varying reports, would indicate problems in cash flow between periods.

Or the change may be a recurring seasonal fact for your company. This should be noted in your report. Customer conditions may affect the current ratio by season as well. For example, if your sales are made predominantly on account, and most of your customers experience seasonal variation, it will be reflected in your own current ratio.

Quick Assets Ratio Trend

The current ratio may be difficult to report with consistency, because inventories are physically counted only once per year. So your analysis may be limited to a quick assets ratio (current assets without inventory, divided by current liabilities).

You are given the following summary:

Quarter	Current Assets	Current Liabilities
Mar 31	$62,000	$58,300
Jun 30	81,400	78,600
Sep 30	92,300	89,100
Dec 31	58,600	60,600

You calculate these quick assets ratios:

Mar 31	1.06 to 1
Jun 30	1.04 to 1
Sep 30	1.04 to 1
Dec 31	0.97 to 1

The ratio is consistent throughout the first three quarters. Is the December 31 unfavorable result indicative of a trend? You would have to look at ratios for past years, and take into account seasonal factors, any extraordinary items adjusted for the annual closing of the books, or other outside influences.

analysis of current ratio

Jan	1.3 to 1
Feb	1.8 to 1
Mar	2.1 to 1
Apr	2.7 to 1 (A)
May	2.6 to 1
Jun	2.9 to 1
Jul	3.3 to 1
Aug	2.8 to 1
Sep	2.9 to 1
Oct	2.4 to 1 (B)
Nov	1.8 to 1
Dec	1.4 to 1

(A) Signals the beginning of high volume
and cash flow period

(B) Signals the beginning of low volume
and cash flow period

Turnover in Working Capital Trend

Working capital is sales divided by current assets less current liabilities. You want to know, on average, how frequently working capital is "turned over" during a period of time. That number demonstrates how effectively the company is controlling working capital to produce sales. An unfavorable trend might develop when the volume of total sales increases rapidly, and the company becomes lax in its control of accounts receivable. For example:

Quarter	Total Sales	Current Assets	Current Liabilities
Mar 31	$2,300,000	$532,600	$315,700
Jun 30	2,482,000	744,700	442,400
Sep 30	2,933,000	884,100	486,800
Dec 31	3,245,000	910,000	446,300

With this information, you can calculate the following turnover in working capital:

Mar 31	10.6 times
Jun 30	8.2 times
Sep 30	7.4 times
Dec 31	7.0 times

What conclusions can be drawn from this? If you look at the current ratio alone, the trend is quite positive, increasing from 1.69 to 1 (March) to 2.04 to 1 (December). But the turnover in working capital has slowed during the same period. When this happens, it's a sign that an increasing portion of current assets are becoming tied up in too-high levels of noncash items such as accounts receivable and inventory. Perhaps the accounts receivable balance is edging higher each month, and the average account is taking longer to collect—a common problem in expanding sales periods. Or average inventory levels may be higher, another factor in a period when sales are expanding.

Possible solutions to the turnover trend might be to tighten policies to improve the time required to collect receivables, or to control growth in inventory levels to a ratio related to the increases in volume of sales.

When this turnover improves—when the number of turns increases in a period—that is a sign that control of working capital is being improved.

Inventory Turnover Trend

The purpose of tracking inventory turnover is to watch for signs that stock is not being efficiently replaced. The turnover computation is an average, based on dividing average inventory levels by the cost of goods sold.

Suppose that during the last year, your company has experienced a substantial increase in total sales volume. This has also led to higher inventory levels. An analysis completed each month reveals the following information:

Month	Cost of Goods Sold	Average Inventory	Turnover
Jan	$ 843,800	$244,500	3.45 times
Feb	864,100	265,800	3.25 times
Mar	938,300	301,800	3.11 times
Apr	1,007,800	315,600	3.19 times
May	994,300	333,400	2.98 times
Jun	1,050,700	355,900	2.95 times

This trend indicates that inventory levels are higher than they should be, and that stock is not being moved as efficiently as in the past. That means a higher cost of storage and poorer use of working capital.

Possible control measures include oversight of purchasing procedures, analysis of physical counts to identify unnecessary or excessive items in stock, and identification of minimum and maximum acceptable turnover rates.

Debt/Equity Ratio Trend

Your company has been increasing its debt levels during the past three years, according to the following summary:

	Liabilities	Net Worth
One year ago	$1,586,500	$2,735,700
Two years ago	1,347,400	2,450,000
Three years ago	980,000	1,582,900

At first glance, a reviewer might express concern that the level of debt has increased at this rate. However, these were profitable years; net worth grew because of retention of profits. The debt/equity ratio (computed by dividing liabilities by tangible net worth) does not show an unfavorable trend. Compared to equity, the level of debt is consistent within a close range.

One year ago	58.0%
Two years ago	55.0%
Three years ago	61.9%

Return on Sales Trend

You may establish a return on sales trend analysis using one of two methods: (1) comparing current months or quarters to the same months or quarters in previous years, or (2) comparing 12-month moving averages of gross sales and net profits. Watching the trend of net profits as a factor of gross sales can lead to incorrect conclusions when small periods of time are analyzed. A change in profits may be due to correcting adjustments, for example, or seasonal factors.

    As an example of how results can mislead, say you gather the following information:

Period	Gross Sales	Net Profit	Return
1st Qtr	$16.45 million	$1.43 million	8.7%
2nd Qtr	21.88 million	1.81 million	8.3
3rd Qtr	43.04 million	3.79 million	8.8
4th Qtr	18.62 million	1.38 million	7.4

    Before concluding that the fourth quarter's results are negative, you should review similar results for the fourth quarter in past years. Also look for any adjustments made to profits during the fourth quarter. For example, in preparation for the end of the year, an internal audit might have resulted in adjustment entries applying to other quarters. A report and analysis of trends in return on sales should be adjusted to explain seasonal variation and allow for extraordinary adjustments.

Return on Capital Trend

This trend should be reported on a 12-month basis only. Net profits are divided by the beginning balance of equity, adjusted for any interim additions of capital.

As you interpret changes in the ratio, be sure to take into account certain cautions. A decline in the rate of return might be the result of changes in corporate policy. For example, instead of paying out earnings in increased dividends, management might choose to retain profits and invest in market expansion. The result: higher current expenses and a lower return on capital, with the expectation of higher future profits.

Also, significant changes in the rate of return will result when one-time adjustments are made to the books. Finally, be aware that movements in the trend may not be significant in isolation. You must interpret the trend in comparison to a number of years.

Collection Ratio Trend

The collection ratio, computed by dividing average accounts receivable by average daily sales, tells you how long it takes to collect receivables due. Analyzing this ratio over time tells you how efficiently you are managing cash flow.

For example, your company tracks the collection ratio each month, based on the moving average of the last 12 months' average accounts receivable and daily sales. The following results are reported:

Month	Average Receivables	Average Daily Sales
Jan	$632,500	$14,580
Feb	688,600	15,310
Mar	737,400	15,730
Apr	760,900	15,770
May	772,100	15,400
Jun	778, 500	15,247

Sales volume is increasing through the first six months of the year, and so is the average daily sales. The collection ratio, though, demonstrates that it is taking longer to collect receivables each month:

Jan	43.4 days
Feb	45.0 days
Mar	46.9 days
Apr	48.2 days
May	50.1 days
Jun	51.1 days

This trend calls for corrective action, including strict enforcement of collection procedures. There is a tendency, during periods of increased volume, to relax this effort. The result is an unfavorable increase in the collection ratio. When major contributors to the problem are identified, it might be necessary to limit further extension of credit to avoid future bad debts, and to increase contact with past-due accounts.

When control procedures are put into effect, allow time for the trend to improve. The effects will not show up for two to three months. Looking back, you will be able to spot the height of the negative trend, the date you identified the problem and began corrective action, and the date the ratio was reversed and stabilized; see "Analysis of Collection Ratio."

EFFECTIVE TREND REPORTS

With reliable information at hand—accurate data, adjusted when necessary, covering an appropriate time period—you are in a position to analyze the trends that emerge. But that's only half the job. Now you must consolidate your analysis into a report for management's review and action. Your presentation should be made in three steps (see "The Three-Part Trend Report").

1. *Correct presentation.* Information must be presented as clearly as possible, combining a narrative description of the most important point and supported with a straightforward numerical summary.

2. *Interpretation and causes.* A report should do more than simply

analysis of collection ratio

	DAYS	
Jan	39.6	
Feb	38.8	
Mar	39.5	
Apr	40.2	
May	42.4	
Jun	44.6	(A)
Jul	41.3	(B)
Aug	41.5	
Sep	41.0	
Oct	39.4	(C)
Nov	39.4	
Dec	39.1	

(A) The trend is unfavorable, as the average collection period is increasing

(B) Collection policies are tightened and enforced

(C) The ratio is reduced to an acceptable level

present information; it should also explain why a trend is occurring. Your report should include an attempt to discover where the company has gone wrong. For instance, if you've been tracking decreasing return on sales, you might conclude that several general expense accounts have been increasing. It is common that in periods of expansion, management does not exercise proper control over spending, resulting in lower margins of profit.

3. Solutions. The report concludes with recommendations that should correct the problem. Solutions should be precise, accompanied with historical support. For example, if you are attempting to explain that there is a need for control of expenses, you should include a summary of increases over the period of time, and suggest controls that might be put into effect.

Memory Jogger: The Three-Part Trend Report

There are three parts in effective trend reporting.
1. Correct presentation.
   a. Summarize the facts.
   b. Include factual support.
   c. Explain briefly.
2. Interpretation and causes.
   a. State what's significant.
   b. Investigate.
   c. Identify and explain reasons.
3. Solutions.
   a. Explain what has occurred.
   b. Include historical evidence.
   c. Offer positive actions.

BEYOND THE TREND

While properly prepared trend analysis is an excellent tool for measurement, it is not the final word. Remember these practical points about the process of using trend information:

1. Identifying the problem and likely solution is not enough. The proper action must be taken to reverse negative trends and encourage positive ones. One pitfall is to become so involved in trend watching that no effort is put into action.

2. Some situations can be identified but not corrected. They may be beyond your control or too severe or chronic to be solved.

3. Once you know how to identify and communicate a trend, the easy part is done. Correcting a problem is where the hard task of good management must begin.

4. Descriptions and examples tend to make the process of trend analysis appear relatively simple. In fact, trends do not always move in one direction, but tend to alternate unpredictably. Recognizing a solid trend requires analysis over a long period, often more than one year.

5. Finally, even the most diligent detective work, the most professionally prepared report, and the most creative proposals for action will not always lead to positive results. As often as not, the solutions you propose will depend on the active participation of others. That may be prevented by perceived priorities, lack of understanding of the process, political considerations, or inability.

As the preparer of a report and the communicator of facts, you are limited by these realities. A trend analysis may provide needed information to others; it will not always cause them to act. So view this valuable reporting tool in perspective. It will improve your value to the company, help you to alter those matters within your direct control, better your understanding of your own job, and increase your comprehension of the factors that influence success and failure.

The work project begins on page 86.

WORK PROJECT

1. Average production per employee in the manufacturing division was 24 units per shift two years ago. Last year, the average increased to 27, and this year to 31. Write a brief narrative statement about this trend.

_____

_____

_____

2. Sales per representative were $14,800 per month on average last summer. But by December, it had fallen to $11,300. Looking at the last three years, you realize that seasonal averages have always fallen between 30 and 35% by the end of the year.

   a. Is this year's change favorable or unfavorable? ....
   b. Write a statement explaining the trend.

_____

_____

_____

3. Revenue and expenses for the last four years were:

	Revenues	Expenses
Last year	$7,715,000	$5,429,000
Two years ago	7,103,000	5,092,000
Three years ago	6,845,000	4,993,000
Four years ago	6,350,000	4,699,000

a. Is this trend favorable or unfavorable, and why? _____

_____

b. Write a brief explanation of the trend in expenses in relation to sales for the last four years.

_____

_____

_____

4. In reviewing your company's financial statement, you collect the following information:

Month	Current Assets	Current Liabilities
Jul	$410,600	$200,500
Aug	501,100	265,300
Sep	488,100	274,700
Oct	423,400	222,300
Nov	452,900	261,700
Dec	423,600	235,900

Prepare a summary of the trend in the current ratio and identify three possible causes for the change.

_____

_____

_____

_____

_____

_____

6

Charts and Graphs

"A picture shows me at a glance what it takes dozens of pages to expound."

—Ivan Sergeyevich Turgenev

Executives in one engineering firm met each month for a budget review. For several months running, the reports were positive but the presentation was bland. One month, as the accountant rose to give his report, one vice president whispered, "The news must be really good this month. He's going to make the presentation with an overhead projector."

There is one business axiom that says you should use charts and graphs only when you have good news—or something to sell. But in fact, whether you have good or bad news, you communicate more effectively by presenting information in a visual mode. There is nothing as uninteresting as a series of numbers, even when their significance is great. And if it's uninteresting, most people will give the list so little attention they miss the point. But reduce those same numbers to a graph, and the significance immediately becomes obvious to everyone.

The usefulness of visual aids is not limited to presentations of financial results; the large graph of sales or profits on the wall behind the president's desk is only one form of graphic presentation. We all express information in mathematical terms, and our progress is measured by supervisors by the same means. A graph simply makes those measurements visual. Some examples:

1. The foreman on a production line tracked defects by the week, giving his crew a visual goal of reducing the graph line over time. Other shifts picked up on the idea. Within two months, defects were reduced overall by more than 30%.

2. The supervisor of a word processing department charted the volume of assignments over a six-month period. She recognized a pattern tied to a monthly cycle, and was thus able to anticipate high-volume periods and better prepare for them.

3. The manager of customer service graphed the time required to resolve customer complaints or answer questions that came in by phone or by mail. The goal was to reduce the average time by improving response and followup. The graph helped pinpoint problems.

Charts and graphs can enliven any kind of report, whether it is in written or oral form. But in all cases, follow these guidelines:

1. Find appropriate places to use charts or graphs. Strike a balance between narrative and visual presentation.
2. Remember that too many visuals will distract from the impact of your message.
3. Perfect visual reports take time and are usually unnecessary. If you don't have an art department or a draftsperson available, a modest hand-drawn graph or typed chart will do.

EFFECTIVE USE OF CHARTS

The easiest form of visual aid is the chart. You will find many opportunities to balance your presentations through a combination of charts and narratives. For example, say you are reporting on the number of employees in your department this year and last year. You could summarize the information with a chart alone:

Data Processing Department—
Summary of Employees on Staff

Classification	Last Year	This Year
Senior analysts	8	5
Programmers	3	7
Assistant programmers	9	6
Systems analysts	1	5
Systems liaisons	5	7
Operations staff	16	26
Clerical support	12	18
Total	54	74

This chart gives only the numerical information, and that is the least useful form of reporting. An alternative is to present the entire report in a strictly narrative format:

The data processing department increased the size of its staff from 54 employees last year to 74 this year.

Significant increases included operations staff, which grew by 10 people, caused by greater support requirements during the conversion period; and clerical support, which increased by 6 people.

Increases in programming and systems analyst staffs were partially offset by decreases in the number of systems analysts and assistant programmers.

The problem with this all-narrative format is that the information is less clear. The preparer made a commendable attempt to stay away from a lifeless summary using numbers alone, but ended up obscuring the information and giving the reader no indication of causes.

A third alternative is to combine visual and narrative information. The narrative portion should be reserved for true analysis, and should *not* be a mere repeat of the numbers.

Data Processing Department—
Summary of Employees on Staff

Classification	Last Year	This Year
Increases		
Operations staff	16	26
Clerical support	12	18
Other net changes	26	30
Total	54	74

The 37% increase in department staff was the result of significant growth in work load, related to the companywide system conversion. However, the majority of staff growth was confined to clerical and operations staffs.

We consider the change an indication of positive cost controls over salaries paid to senior staff members, notably senior analysts and systems analysts (staffs increased by only 1 employee, net).

While the number of employees increased 37%, the total payroll for the department has grown by only 17%.

The chart was reduced to the key facts and the narrative was confined to an analysis of results. This anticipates, and answers, the questions that management would naturally ask: Why are we adding so many people to that department? Isn't it inefficient to increase salaries so drastically? What kind of control are we exercising over the level of new-hires in this department?

Note that in this example some of the data were not used. It is not always necessary—or relevant—to include in a chart all the information you receive. You can move the full information to the back of your report, if you think someone will need to see more details. For example, in commenting on financial results, you can attach a complete financial statement, and include only a summarized chart within the body of your report.

Summary of Operations
For the Year Ended 1987

Total sales	$123,480,500
Cost of goods sold	74,535,200
Gross profit	48,945,300
Operating expenses	39,006,900
Net profit	9,938,400

A summarized chart allows the reader to see at a glance what is occurring and to concentrate on your narrative comments. If your narrative contains too much analysis, you need more visual aids; in those cases, summarize as much as possible to clarify your comments.

Charts are useful tools in most types of reporting, especially when there is a great deal of financial or statistical information to convey. Graphs can take your reporting and communication a step further, making purely financial information both clear and visual.

FUNDAMENTALS OF GOOD GRAPHS

Graphs are visual representation of information. Good graphs make your presentation come alive, and they help your audience (or readers) grasp the main ideas quickly.

Three Essentials

The first question anyone has when looking at a graph is, "What does this mean?" So every graph must contain three things:

1. A descriptive title.
2. Footnotes or annotation as needed.
3. Proper scaling.

The title is essential. Just as any kind of report needs a label, a visual aid must first be properly named. The title should identify the factors on the graph and the time involved. It can be quite simple, even when a complex arrangement of information is involved, such as:

Two-Year Trend in Sales
Gross Profit Analysis, One Year
Average Orders Placed, Six Months

When you are preparing a graph, make sure the title is clear. If you can't work in all the necessary information, you will have to add footnotes or other annotation. These should be used only when necessary to qualify information, especially if the absence of explanation might mislead a reviewer. Examples:

Costs include one-time adjustment for change in inventory valuation.
Average includes sales representatives no longer with the company.
Prior year restated for change in fiscal year.

"Scaling" refers to the dimensions into which information in the graph is organized. There are usually two scales involved, such as "value" and "time." They appear along two sides of the graph, one vertical and one horizontal.

For example, you are preparing a graph that shows net profits over a period of one year. In most graphs, value is shown from the top to the bottom and time moves from left to right. See "Correct Scaling" for example.

The scales in this graph give all the information anyone needs to understand what it represents. Down the left side, the amounts are indicated in thousands of dollars ($000). Along the bottom, the time is indicated by quarter.

The distance between values is always equal. If this rule is not followed, the significance of the graph will be distorted. For example, imagine how differently a trend line would appear if the following breakdown of scales was used (see "Incorrect Scaling").

The value scale has spacing of $100,000 for the three top values but $25,000 for the remainder. And the time values, while given visually equal spacing on the graph, begin with quarterly divisions and then revert to months.

correct scaling

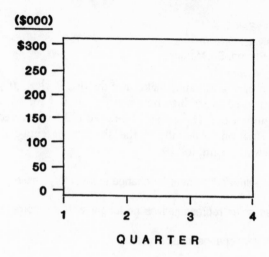

incorrect scaling

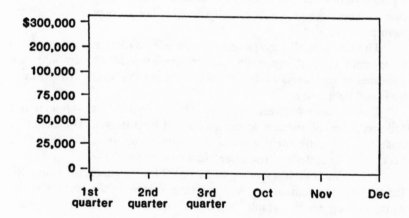

In this second example, the trend line will not accurately represent what has occurred. Whenever you review a graph prepared by someone else, determine that the scale is consistent. If it is not, the visual representation itself is inaccurate.

Many graphs compare two different types of information, such as sales for two different years, orders placed by two regions, or sales and direct costs. When this occurs, two different value scales may be used, with perhaps one at the left and the other at the right. When values cross over one another, the trend lines are easier to read if you use different types of lines. See "Sales and Costs, 1987" for an example.

Common Mistakes

Since the purpose of visual aids is to clarify information, a confusing graph is a failure. The hardest thing to do—and the most important—is to make sure your graph portrays the information accurately.

For example, the marketing vice president of one company prepared a graph from the following information:

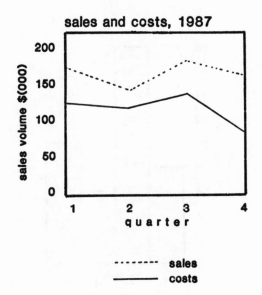

Calendar Quarter	Number of Sales Orders
1	13,450
2	15,901
3	16,838
4	18,560

He designed a graph showing the *percentage increase* by quarter. (The first quarter's orders grew by 8% over the previous quarter, the second quarter by 18%, the third by 6%, and the fourth by 10%.) His graph is shown here as "Sales Growth, by Percentage."

The information is not represented in the best possible way, because it does not show immediately that the volume in orders is, in fact, on

sales growth by percentage

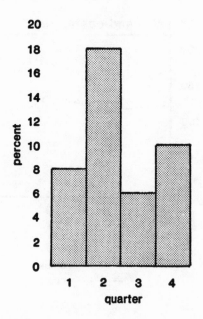

the increase. At first glance, you could easily misinterpret this graph as showing a *decline* in orders during the third quarter.

If it is important to illustrate the increase each quarter, the graph should show progressive growth. Starting from a base of zero (the previous year's fourth quarter), an accurate graph would show the accumulated growth (see "Sales Growth, Accumulated").

This presentation of the information, with such a dramatic curve in growth, looks very impressive—but it doesn't accurately reflect the real volume of orders. The best way to represent this positive trend on a graph is to show the actual number of orders, accumulated by quarter (see "New Orders Placed.")

The danger in developing graphs is the possibility that the end result will not show what was intended. Anyone creating visual aids should be diligently aware of this pitfall. A confusing graph is worse than no graph at all.

Be on guard also against:

1. Confusing or inaccurate title.
2. Lack of required footnotes or annotation.
3. Excessive information.
4. Inconsistent or unclear scaling.
5. Inappropriate graph for the subject.
6. A derivative form of information that distorts significance.

Those who review graphs are subject to another common error: focusing too quickly on the reported information (the trend line, for

sales growth, accumulated

	INCREASE	ACCUMULATED GROWTH
1st quarter	8%	8%
2nd quarter	18	26
3rd quarter	6	32
4th quarter	10	42

new orders placed

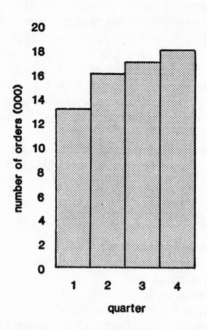

example). It is a mistake to try to absorb the significance of a graph by looking first at the trend line and *then* looking at the other components of the graph. You can help, especially if your report is oral, by calling attention to the elements of the graph in the proper sequence: the title, additional notes, scaling, and finally, the actual results reported.

THREE KINDS OF GRAPHS

Information can be summarized in three types of graphs:

1. The line graph, used to demonstrate change over time.
2. The bar graph, used to compare related information and relative significance.

3. The circle graph (also called a pie chart), which shows the relationship between information and each segment's contribution to the whole.

The selection of one visual over another depends partly on the nature of information, and partly on the preference of the individual preparing it. Sometimes, for consistency's sake, a visual is prepared the same way as in the past. But regardless of the type of graph, the rules are identical: It must be properly titled, the scale must be consistent, and any additional information must be included.

Line Graph

The line graph is the most familiar type. It is built on a square or rectangle, with a scale of value (such as dollar amount) up and down the sides of the square, and a second factor (such as time) along the bottom. See "Line Graph—Two Values."

Example: You are asked to prepare a report showing the volume of sales in the eastern division. You gather the following information for last year:

line graph – two values

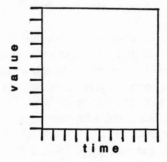

EASTERN SALES DIVISION

Jan	$323,800	Jul	$446,700
Feb	318,400	Aug	454,800
Mar	331,600	Sep	441,500
Apr	362,900	Oct	380,600
May	401,400	Nov	341,700
Jun	420,300	Dec	329,100

To create a line graph, you must first determine the scale. The graph should be compact enough to fit on a half page, but broad enough to show the significance of changes over time. The half-page size will be large enough for most graphs. If you decide to use one line per $10,000, you will need to build a graph with no fewer than 46 lines (the largest value is $454,800), which is too large for an efficient graph. But if you select $50,000 as your scale value, the entire graph can fit into 10 lines (see "Graph Design, Step 1").

Once the best scale has been established, you can draw up the preliminary outline. List the dollar value down the left side, and write in the time factors along the bottom. In this case, you will have 10 dollar value scales and 12 time values (months) (see "Graph Design, Step 2").

Next, plot the graph for each dollar value and time. For example, in the column for "January," place a dot on the row approximating $323,800 (see "Graph Design, Step 3").

Once you have plotted the entire 12 months, connect the dots to create your line. As a last step, type in your scales and label, as in "The Completed Line Graph."

The line graph can be used to show not only the trend of one factor, but a comparison. For example, suppose you are asked to do the same assignment but in addition to compare monthly sales for the division to sales levels during the previous year. This will show the change from one year to the other, as well as the trend during the current year.

This technique is best used when the lines of the graph will not cross one another. For example, if last year's sales were consistently less than this year's level, the line graph would be appropriate. If they

graph design – step 1

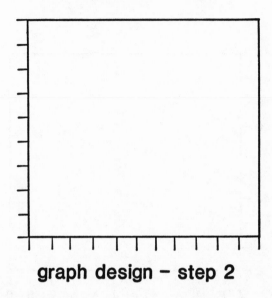

graph design – step 2

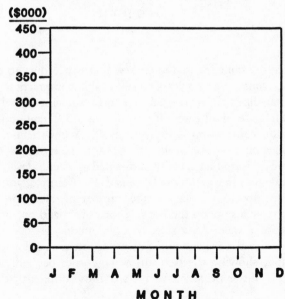

graph design – step 3

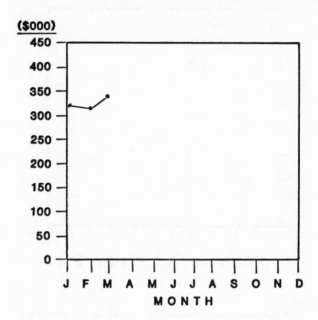

approximate the same levels, the lines will cross, leading to confusion. In that case, combining two years on one graph is impractical.

If separate line graphs are used to report results for several divisions, use the same scale in all cases. If you design a different scale for each graph, a valid comparison is more difficult. A low-volume division's results, placed on a broader scale, may seem to be more positive than a high-volume division that actually performed at a better level.

The scale on a line graph can be mixed. For example, you may want to show both divisional sales and the number of sales representatives. You could create a scale on the left side for dollars and one on the right for number of people. As a rule, though, mixing factors on a graph tends to confuse the reader, while revealing little. A solution: Make a second graph, showing the trend in average sales per individual. The scale would be different, as an average will move differently than a total

the completed line graph

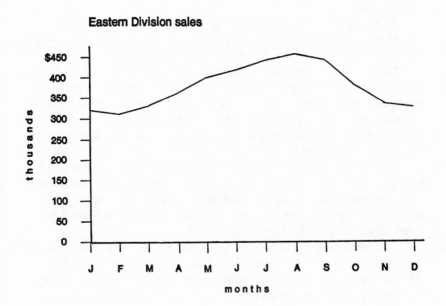

Eastern Division sales

for the division. In the interest of clarity, separating the information and discussing it elsewhere in the report makes sense.

A graph should always be accompanied with a brief explanation. While the purpose of a visual aid is to make a trend more visible, a comment is almost always needed, too.

> Eastern division sales are summarized on the accompanying graph. The seasonal volume growth from May through September was the best for this division during the last four years. Total sales for the year were 14% higher than during the previous 12 months.

The Bar Graph

The second type of graph is appropriate for comparing two or more types of information. The bar graph can be formatted vertically or horizontally.

Example: Rather than reporting sales for only one division, you are asked to report on results for all three. A single vertical bar graph can be used to combine results and still keep them distinct.

Start by identifying the appropriate scale, just as you did with the line graph. In this case, it may be clearer to combine volume into quarterly totals. You're not merely showing a trend, but an overall comparison, so quarterly totals may better reflect what has occurred between divisions. This requires a different scale, as the dollar amounts are greater. For example, you might set the scale at $100,000 per line.

Each period will be represented with a bar denoting value. So for each period, there will be three bars, one for each division. Decide how wide the quarterly bar will be, and draw your boxes to scale. Finally, label the first set of bars (it is not necessary to write in a label every time), as shown in "The Vertical Bar Graph."

The information can also be presented horizontally, which some people prefer. For some types of information, it is easier to perceive the significance of values in comparison on a horizontal scale. For example, you are reporting on production levels in several different plants. You have this data to work with:

	Units Produced	
Plant Location	*Last Year*	*This Year*
Watertown	1,714	1,150
Ogdensburg	1,455	1,601
Canton	840	966
Massena	610	682

A horizontal bar chart can be used to highlight the differences, as shown in the example. As always, an explanation should accompany the graph:

Volume of production fell this year in the Watertown plant, the result of equipment breakdowns and a three-month strike.

the vertical bar graph

Sales by division

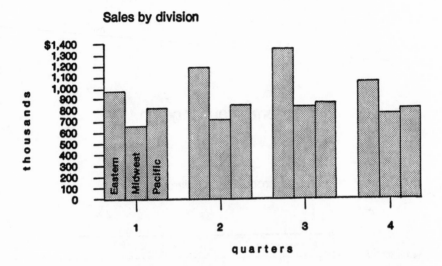

The remaining three plants improved productivity rates, all without significant growth in their costs related to sales or in levels of overhead expenses.

It is often helpful to present a graph, include a brief explanation of trends and causes for change, and then summarize with a chart of the activity, for those who prefer looking at the numbers alone.

The Circle Graph

The third type of graph can be effective for reporting information in greatly summarized form. It is meant as a way to show proportionate contributions of several elements to the whole.

Example: You compile the following information for a report on overhead expenses for the last year:

Salaries and wages	$12,682,513
Advertising and marketing	4,316,810
Rent	3,844,600
Telephone and utilities	1,403,005
Other expenses	6,447,934
Total	$28,694,862

the horizontal bar graph

Units of production by plant

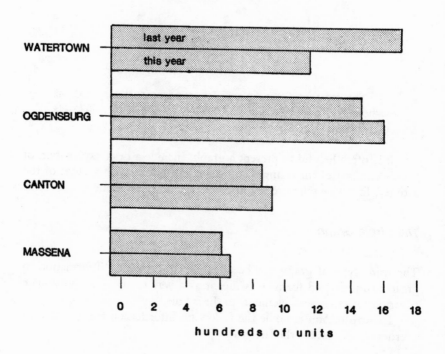

To represent this information with a circle graph, follow these steps:

1. First, break down the information by percentages, and round to the nearest whole percent:

Salaries and wages	44%
Advertising and marketing	15
Rent	13
Telephone and utilities	5
Other expenses	23
Total	100%

2. Compute the degree of each, based on the 360 degrees of a circle, and round to the nearest whole degree:

Salaries and wages	$360 \times .44 = 158$
Advertising and marketing	$360 \times .15 = 54$
Rent	$360 \times .13 = 47$
Telephone and utilities	$360 \times .05 = 18$
Other expenses	$360 \times .23 = 83$
Total	360

3. The graph represents 360 degrees of a circle, so each segment's relative size can be easily computed with a protractor. Salaries and wages represent 158 degrees. Draw your first line from the center of a circle to zero degrees, and another to 158 degrees. Using the last line as a new zero point, go 54 degrees for advertising and marketing. Proceed around the circle in this manner until the entire breakdown has been computed.

4. Label the segments according to the components, as shown in the "Operating Expenses" circle graph.

The narrative accompanying your graph can highlight the significance of the information:

Out of every dollar spent on overhead, 44 cents went to salaries and wages, 15 cents to advertising, and 13 cents to rent. Last year's total expenses of $28.69 million are broken down on the graph below.

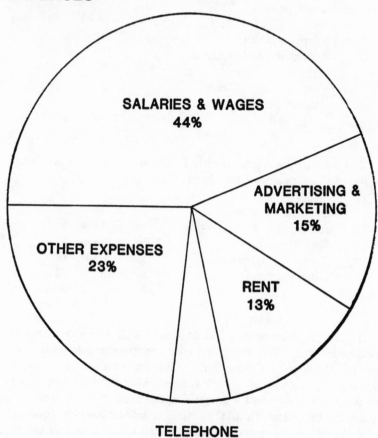

LEGENDS AND FOOTNOTES

To reduce the number of words on the graph itself, or to explain what your scale represents, you can include a coded summary or legend. When you reduce values to length rather than including words or numbers on the graph's scale, the graph becomes purely visual. This tends to stress the comparison while avoiding the distraction of extra information on the graph.

Example: You want to show as visually as possible the significance of growth in the number of customers over three years.

This year	36,000
Last year	21,000
Two years ago	9,000

On a visual graph, the data would look like the "Numerical Growth" example.

This coded technique is also useful in bar graphs comparing different factors. See "Breakdown by Division" graph for an example.

Any technique that adds to clarification or reduces the need for extra words or explanation may be considered in the design of a graph. However, when an explanation is necessary, it can be minimized in one of four ways:

1. *Words in the graph.* If the explanation is minimal, such as the one-word identification of a division or other component, simply add the words on the line or within the appropriate box.

numerical growth

this year	xxxxxxxxxxxx
one year ago	xxxxxxx
two years ago	xxx

legend: x = 3,000

breakdown
by division

xxxxxxxxxxxxxxxxxxx

/////////

+++++++++++++

0   4   8   12   16

legend: x eastern
          / midwest
          + pacific

2. *Caption.* Graphs can be captioned so that the reader knows exactly what the graph explains. For consistency, include titles above the graph itself, and captions below. A caption may explain exactly what is included in the graph, qualify the report, or expand on the title. Some examples:

Title	*Caption*
Sales, One Year	Sales include the new international division, in operation for only eight months this year.
General Expenses by Division	This breakdown does not include interdivisional transfers of expenses. All reported totals are shown where incurred.
Trend in Collections	This graph reports collections on a 12-month moving average basis.

3. *Annotation.* Graphs that need explanation of one or more parts can be annotated (small notes off to the side). For example, the first illustration in this chapter showed eastern division sales for a one-year period. If you believe it is necessary to explain the May to September increase, you could draw a line to the apex of that trend, with a note to the side, reading "seasonal increase." In some cases, proper use of

annotation can get around any need for narratives accompanying the graph.

    4. Footnotes. If annotation would be too distracting, include an annotation line from the point in your graph, going to a circled letter. Then, beneath the graph, type in your referenced footnotes. With this method, you can include a large number of notes and still leave the graph clear and uncluttered.

DRAWING YOUR GRAPHS

Have you stayed away from graphs because you cannot draw well? Don't let that stop you. Your graphs do not have to be perfect, as long as the information they present is clear. You can draw acceptable graphs with a black felt tip or ballpoint pen and a ruler, and fill in details, scales, captions, and legends with your typewriter.

    To ensure complete accuracy, use grid paper. A very light blue grid will not reproduce in most printing and duplication processes, including many photocopy machines. If you want to improve the appearance of titles, experiment with press-on lettering systems, available in any art supply store. The letters are lined up and rubbed onto paper with a burnisher or a pencil tip. It will take a little practice, but makes a lot of difference in the quality of your graphs.

    Being able to prepare passable graphs is a very useful skill. Don't depend on an art department or someone else in your company to produce quality graphics for you. Many of your communications are prepared under pressure, and you won't have time to wait for someone else.

WORK PROJECT

    1. You must construct a line graph showing results of production levels over a two-year period. Your range of values will be units produced, which range up to 24,000. To minimize the height and length of the graph, what is a practical scale?

a. For value? _____

b. For time? _____

2. You want to make a circle graph to show the breakdown of your advertising budget by division. The total budget is assigned 47% to Eastern, 34% to Midwest, and 19% to Pacific. Compute the degrees on the circle that each division is assigned.

_____

_____

_____

3. Use a compass to draw a circle and a protractor to figure degrees. Then, using the information in Question 2, convert the circle into a circle graph to show the advertising budget breakdown.

7

Calculations of Interest

"It was an awful sight of money when it was all piled up. Well, Judge Thatcher he took it and put it out at interest, and it fetched us a dollar a day apiece all year round—more than a body could tell what to do with."

—Mark Twain, *The Adventures of Huckleberry Finn*

The president of one company believed that borrowing money is a necessary evil. "Lenders," he explained, "are like obnoxious in-laws. You don't especially like them, but to survive the relationship, you have to pay some interest—sometimes a lot more interest than you feel they really deserve."

Companies are run on capitalization, which comes from two sources—equity and debt. Equity—the money people put into a company when they buy its stock—is not always enough to finance operations, so a responsible and balanced capitalization plan can and often should include borrowing money from outside sources. Going into debt is smart as long as the profits generated from the use of borrowed funds are greater than the interest that must be paid.

The most apt description of borrowing is the renting of money, and the interest is the rent. Calculations of interest involve three elements: the principal amount, a rate, and the amount of time. Principal, the amount borrowed, is the basis for all interest charges. The rate is expressed as a percentage of the principal. The time involved will determine the total amount that will be paid on the loan.

113

Time may be less than one year, or more. The distinction is important, because the rate is always expressed annually. A 14% loan will mean a charge of 14% per year, or per annum. Interest rates usually are expressed in percentage form, 14%, for example. They can also be shown as decimals: .14, or 14 one-hundredths.

The best way to understand how interest is calculated is to reduce it to a formula.

$$I = P \times R \times T$$

Where

I = Interest
P = Principal
R = Rate
T = Time

Example: Your company purchases a photocopy machine costing $5,000. The manufacturer agrees to deliver today with payment due in one year, with 14% interest. Remember the formula for calculation of interest:

$$I = P \times R \times T$$
$$I = \$5,000 \times 0.14 \times 1$$
$$I = \$700$$

SIMPLE INTEREST

There are several variations of interest calculations. Simple interest is a charge based on the principal amount *only*. With compound interest, you end up paying on an outstanding balance so that, in effect, you pay interest on interest. This will be shown in more detail later on in this chapter.

In this example, the photocopy manufacturer agrees to carry the balance for one year. But what if you negotiate a two-year deal? What happens in the second year will determine whether it is a compound or simple interest loan. Interest for the first year is $700, so the balance due after one year is $5,700 (that is, assuming no payments have been made). The next question is, will interest for the second year be computed on only the original $5,000 (simple interest), or on $5,700 (compound interest)?

The calculation for simple interest for two years is:

$$I = \$5,000 \times 0.14 \times 2$$
$$I = \$1,400$$

To figure the total amount of repayment for simple interest, you simply add the principal of $5,000 to the total interest due, $1,400. So a loan of $5,000 with 14% simple interest, due in two years, requires a payment of $6,400. Expressed as a formula, this is:

$$P + (P \times R \times T)$$
$$\$5,000 + (\$5,000 \times 0.14 \times 2)$$
$$\$5,000 + \$1,400 = \$6,400$$

If you multiply the principal amount instead of adding it again, you can shorten the calculation of total repayment even more.

$$P[1 + (R \times T)]$$

In this abbreviated form, you can cut out one step in the repayment calculation and end up with the same answer:

$$\$5,000 [1 + (0.14 \times 2)] = \$6,400$$

Remember, interest doesn't always apply for periods of one year or more. In these cases, the time factor is a fraction. Since 1 represents one full year, the months are portions of 1. What if the photocopy manufacturer will carry the debt only for three months? A $5,000 debt with interest of 14%, for three months only, will require a payment of:

$$\$5,000 [1 + (0.14 \times 3/12)] = \$5,175$$

The 3/12 represents three months of twelve, and could also be expressed in its reduced form, 1/4. The interest is still 14%, but for a period less than one year. An annual rate of 14% is the same as 3.5% over three months.

Another variation: If the time of the loan is 15 months at simple interest, the repayment formula could be expressed in two ways:

$$\$5,000 \, [1 + (0.14 \times 15/12)]$$

or:

$$\$5,000 \, [1 + (0.14 \times 1.25)]$$

Either way, 15 months are the same as 1 1/4 periods, and the answer is $5,875.

You can prove this answer by checking the previous examples. You know that interest for one year is $700 ($5,000 × 0.14), and you know that interest for three months is $175 ($5,000 × 0.035). If you add the principal and both simple interest calculations together, you prove the answer:

$$\$5,000 + \$700 + \$175 = \$5,875$$

COMPOUND CALCULATIONS

Simple interest rarely applies in management calculations. It is more likely that a loan or a deferred payment agreement will be made with compound interest. When you compound, you are calculating interest on interest. In the examples given above, an annual compound interest rate of 14% would have been done differently. The first year would have been identical to simple interest:

$$\$5,000 \times 1.14 = \$5,700$$

But the second year, because it would be compounded, would treat the balance of $5,700 as a new principal base:

$$\$5,700 \times 1.14 = \$6,498$$

You can see the effect of interest on interest by breaking this out into different sections:

Interest, first year:

$$\$5,000 \times 14\% = \$700$$

Interest, second year:

$$\$5,000 \times 14\% = \$700$$

Interest on interest:

$$\$700 \times 14\% = \$98$$
$$\text{Total compound interest} = \$1,498$$

This compounding makes a big difference over several periods. In this two-year example, the difference is only $98. But depending upon the method of compounding and the amount of the loan, the dollars can add up quickly; see "Annual Compounding." So it is important to question the wisdom of too much debt. Is the cost of interest worth the delay in repayment? You'll find that it isn't always smart to use other people's money.

It is a basic mathematical certainty that the more periods involved in

annual compounding		
	INTEREST	PRINCIPAL
original loan		$ 5,000
year 1	$ 700	5,700
year 2	798	6,498
year 3	910	7,408
year 4	1,037	8,445
year 5	1,182	9,627
year 6	1,348	10,975

a calculation of compound interest, the higher the total cost of the loan. As you build interest into principal, the base gets higher with each additional period. That's the consequence of interest on interest, for the borrower. And there's another point of view: that of a lender or investor. Your money, left on deposit in an interest-bearing account, gathers value with each compound period. So interest can be looked at as an expense for the borrower, or as a source of growing income to the lender/ investor. The significance of an interest rate itself becomes obvious when an amount of money is compounded over many years. For example, see "Compound Interest Comparison."

compound interest comparison
(compounded annually)

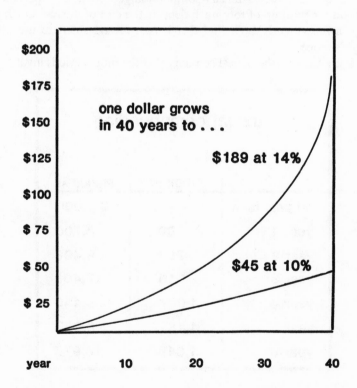

Compounding can be expressed in a formula that is similar to that for simple interest (with C as the cost):

$$C = P (1 + R)^T$$

The total cost (C) of the loan equals the principal (P) multiplied by 1 plus the interest rate (R), multiplied by the number of compound periods, or time (T). In the case of the photocopy machine, assume your $5,000 balance was financed at 14% interest for three years, compounded annually:

$$C = \$5,000 (1 + 0.14)^3 = \$7,408$$

If you were figuring interest for many periods, this would take a great deal of time and tedious computation. Interest rate tables (see sample) greatly simplify things. The factors given in the tables are used in calculations, removing the necessity for working out lengthy multiplications. Using the sample rates in the table, you could do the following calculations quite easily:

Principal	Rate	Periods	Factor	Total Cost
$ 5,000	12%	4	1.573519	$ 7,867.60
2,000	16	5	2.100342	4,200.68
6,000	12	2	1.254400	7,526.40
10,000	14	6	2.194973	21,949.73
1,000	10	3	1.331000	1,331.00

Having the table allows a quick total cost computation. As long as you know the elements, you can get around the need for an extended formula.

The tables work for interest compounded more frequently than once per year, too. The only adjustment needed is in the rate. For example, if your $5,000 loan at 14% is compounded every six months, it means you have two periods per year. But the rate is halved, and the formula for the first six-month period is:

$$C = \$5,000 [1 + (0.14 \div 2)] = \$5,350$$

Sample Compound Interest Rate Table

Number of Periods	*10%*	*12%*	*14%*	*16%*
1	1.100000	1.120000	1.140000	1.160000
2	1.210000	1.254400	1.299600	1.345600
3	1.331000	1.404928	1.481544	1.560896
4	1.464100	1.573519	1.688960	1.810639
5	1.610510	1.762342	1.925415	2.100342
6	1.771561	1.973823	2.194973	2.436396

In this first period, the interest is exactly one-half of the straight annual rate of 14%, which is $700. But the rules of compounding work during the second six-month period too:

$$C = \$5,350\,[1 + (0.14 \div 2)] = \$5,724.50$$

This answer can be proved by using the longhand representation of the formula:

$$C = \$5,000\,(1.07)\,(1.07)$$

Other compounding periods are described in the next section.

COMPOUNDING METHODS

Up to now we have been working with compound interest on an annual basis, but interest is not always compounded yearly. Interest compounding for less than one year requires computing a fraction of the annual rate. When the annual rate is 14%, the effective rates for part of a year are:

Monthly	1 month	1/12	1.17%
Quarterly	3 months	3/12 or 1/4	3.50%
Semiannual	6 months	6/12 or 1/2	7.00%

Monthly Compounding

With monthly compounding, you are dealing with twelve separate interest periods, each with 1/12 the annual rate. The difference this makes is apparent when you do the multiple compounding. The long-hand formula to compute the actual effective annual rate of 14% would involve 12 multiplications:

$$(1.0117) \, (1.0117) \, (1.0117) \ldots (1.0117)$$

It can be more easily expressed as:

$$(1.0117)^{12}$$

And in a calculation:

$$C = \$5,000 \, (1 + 0.0117)^{12} = \$5,749$$

You can make the task of calculation easier with the use of interest rate tables. If monthly tables are not available, you can make your own; see "Constructing a Monthly Table." While tables make calculation easier, many people have a great deal of trouble figuring out which type of interest table to use. We will examine the reasons for this and offer solutions in the next chapter. The examples in this chapter should clarify the methods of calculation, so that you will be more comfortable with interest tables. For more explanation, refer to Chapter 9.

Constructing a Monthly Table

To build a table for computing interest compounded monthly, follow these steps:

1. Divide the annual rate by 12 to determine the monthly fraction.
2. Add 1 to the fraction for the first month's factor.
3. Multiply the factor times itself to build the 12-month table.

Monthly Compounding of 14% Annual Interest

Period	1/12	Factor
1	.011667	1.011667
2	.011667	1.023470
3	.011667	1.035411
4	.011667	1.047491
5	.011667	1.059712
6	.011667	1.072076
7	.011667	1.084584
8	.011667	1.097237
9	.011667	1.110039
10	.011667	1.122990
11	.011667	1.136091
12	.011667	1.149346

The method of building a monthly compound chart is shown in the accompanying table, using 14% as an example. The annual percentage rate (APR) in this example is 14.9346% (the factor for the twelfth month, 1.149346). When such a loan is offered, it commonly will be expressed as "14% (14.93% APR)." Stated another way, $1 will grow to $1.149346 in 12 months at 14%, compounded monthly.

Quarterly Compounding

Quarterly compounding works the same way, but with 4 interest periods instead of 12. An annual rate is divided by 4, and there are 4 compounding periods, one each quarter. Divide 14% by 4, for a quarterly rate of 3.5%. In longhand that would be expressed:

$$(1.035) \ (1.035) \ (1.035) \ (1.035)$$

The shorthand version:

$$(1.035)^4$$

The annual percentage rate in this example is 14.7523%, and the $5,000 loan would cost you $5,737.61.

Semiannual Compounding

Semiannual interest is computed using two periods per year. We described the step-by-step process earlier in this chapter. For 14% divide by 2 and multiply the halved rate. In longhand that would be:

$$(1.07)\ (1.07)$$

The shorthand version:

$$(1.07)^2$$

The APR: 14.49%. And you would have to repay $5,724.50.

In summary then, the amount you have to repay is affected not only by the interest rate and the time period, but also by the method of compounding that is used.

$$\$5,000 \times 14\% \text{ annually} = \$5,700.00$$
$$\$5,000 \times 14\% \text{ semiannually} = \$5,724.50$$
$$\$5,000 \times 14\% \text{ quarterly} = \$5,737.61$$
$$\$5,000 \times 14\% \text{ monthly} = \$5,746.73$$

If you were dealing with $5 million instead of $5,000—which you might be in a large corporation—the difference would be quite significant.

Daily Compounding

The last method of compounding is daily. For this, more than for the other methods, you need an interest rate table, because the calculation is so large. And there are two methods: the 365-day year (calendar) and the 360-day year (banking). The method of computation is identical as with the other methods. However, you need 360 or 365 calculations instead of 12, 4, or 2. Daily compounding is more commonly used for savings accounts, and rarely for loans. So a different example will be used to demonstrate.

Interest Rate Table, Daily Compounding (360 days)

(What a $1 deposit will grow to in the future)

| Number of | Annual Percentage Rate | | | |
Years	7.5%	7.75%	8%	8.25%
1	1.0790	1.0817	1.0845	1.0872
2	1.1642	1.1702	1.1761	1.1821
3	1.2562	1.2658	1.2755	1.2852
4	1.3555	1.3693	1.3832	1.3973
5	1.4625	1.4812	1.5001	1.5192
6	1.5781	1.6022	1.6268	1.6517
7	1.7027	1.7332	1.7642	1.7958
8	1.8373	1.8749	1.9133	1.9525
9	1.9824	2.0281	2.0749	2.1228
10	2.1390	2.1939	2.2502	2.3080

Assume you have $2,000 in a savings account paying 8% compounded daily for eight years. What will the compound value be at the end of that period? See the accompanying daily interest rate table for the factors. For eight years at 8%, the factor is 1.9133, so the formula is:

$$\$2{,}000 \times 1.9133 = \$3{,}826.60$$

If the account were compounded quarterly, a different table would be used. The total would have grown to $3,768 (2,000 × 1.884), or $58.60 less. So the more frequent compounding does make a difference over time.

INVESTMENT APPLICATIONS

Return on investment indicates the success of the use of money, whether put into a passive savings account, mutual funds, or the capital of a corporation. Interest calculations are used in virtually all forms of reporting investment results. Because our primary standard for comparison is the rate of return, the concern is with yield—interest on money. Some forms of return—notably dividends and capital gains—are considered separately from interest, but still are a part of the total return.

Example: You are given the assignment of calculating the annual return on an investment your company made in the stock of another company. You find the following data:

Purchase price	$13,525.00
Dividends received	$ 2,028.75
Sale proceeds	$16,375.00
Holding period	38 months

The total profit consists of a capital gain ($16,375.00 less $13,525.00 = $2,850) plus dividends earned, for a total of $4,878.75. The total return is computed by dividing total profit by the original investment:

$$\$4,878.75 \div \$13,525 = 36.07\%$$

Since the holding period was 38 months, the annual profit is actually only 12/38, or 11.39%.

Another application of interest computations arises in financial analysis. For example, on sales of $6.3 million, last year's profits were $502,380 and equity in the company was $8.36 million. Net profits can be expressed in several ways:

As a dollar amount: $502,380
As a return on total sales: 7.97%
As a return on equity: 6.01%

We must review forecasts and budgets in terms of a return on investment. For example, you are given the job of completing this year's departmental budget. In the past, the rate of return has been used as a standard for comparison. You know the historical rate from past financial reports, and can compare it to the present return. So your department's report takes on more significance than the numbers by themselves.

WORK PROJECT

1. Your company plans to enter several short-term financing agreements. You are given the assignment of computing interest for monthly compounding at the nominal annual rate of 8%. Construct an interest rate table showing the effective rate for months 1 through 12.

_____

_____

_____

_____

_____

_____

2. You are estimating rates of return on a number of outstanding loans. Using the formula:

$$\text{Interest} = \text{Principal} \times \text{Rate} \times \text{Time}$$

show the correct equation and compute interest for the following:

a. $5,000 at 7% for 15 months, annual compounding.
b. $1,000 at 6% for 9 months, annual compounding.
c. $800 at 8% for one year, monthly compounding (hint: use the table developed in question 1).
d. $2,000 at 8% for 2 years, simple interest.
e. $1,000 at 6% for 3 years, annual compounding.

3. You have three different time deposit accounts, each paying interest on the 360-day compounding method. Using the compounding table in this chapter, how much will the following grow to?

a. $1,000 at 7.5% in 9 years.   . . . .
b. $6,000 at 8.25% in 2 years.   . . . .
c. $400 at 8% in 7 years.   . . . .

4. Your company expects an 11% return on the use of money. Assuming this is an annual compound rate, compute the effective return for:

a. Two months.   . . . .
b. Three months. . . . .
c. Eight months. . . . .

8

Loan Amortization

"Money is always there, but the pockets change."

—Gertrude Stein

The chief accountant told the assembled executives and managers, "We earned a net profit last year, before interest expense. But interest on outstanding loans took us out of the black column and into the red." When asked what he suggested to correct the problem, he answered, "We're currently negotiating for new loans."

Once a company goes too heavily into debt, it becomes increasingly difficult to escape the burden of interest. In the example above, repayment drained cash flow and ate up profits, and finally the situation broke the organization. In the words of one vice president, "We found ourselves in a no-win situation. We were rearranging deck chairs on the *Titanic*."

In your job as well as in your personal life, you will encounter a number of circumstances when an understanding of amortization will make your task easier. Amortization is the process of reducing a loan's balance over time. For example, you are considering buying a house. To start with, you need to figure out what you can afford. That means estimating monthly payments. Or your company is carrying a debt on its books, and you are asked to break out interest and principal for the next 12 months.

In situations like these, a knowledge of how loans are amortized over many years is valuable and necessary. If you don't understand how to use amortization tables, you must depend upon someone else—a banker or a real estate agent, for example—to tell you the level of monthly payment or the breakdown between principal and interest.

AMORTIZATION TABLES

The easiest way to figure out how large a monthly payment will be required to amortize (pay off) a loan in the period called for, including interest *and* principal payments, is to refer to an interest amortization table. These tables are difficult to use if you do not understand their purpose. That's because they consist of rows and columns of numbers, which make little or no sense until the concept of loan amortization is fully comprehended.

Consider the problem: You take out a bank loan for $20,000 for one year, which is payable at 9%. In order to fully pay off the loan in 12 months, how much must each payment be? The steps are:

1. Look up the table for the correct frequency of payments. For example, if you will make monthly payments, be sure to refer to a monthly amortization table.
2. Find the page for the percentage of interest you are being charged.
3. Find the loan amount on the far left-hand column.
4. Move across to the column for the number of years you have to pay off the loan.

Sample Monthly Amortization Table—9%

Amount	Monthly Payment Required to Amortize a Loan					
	1 Year	5 Years	10 Years	15 Years	20 Years	30 Years
$ 50	4.38	1.04	.64	.51	.45	.41
100	8.75	2.08	1.27	1.02	.90	.81
500	43.73	10.38	6.34	5.08	4.50	4.03
1,000	87.46	20.76	12.67	10.15	9.00	8.05
5,000	437.26	103.80	63.34	50.72	44.99	40.24

10,000	874.52	207.59	126.68	101.43	89.98	80.47
15,000	1311.78	311.38	190.02	152.14	134.96	120.70
20,000	1749.03	415.17	253.36	202.86	179.95	160.93
25,000	2186.29	518.96	316.69	253.57	224.94	201.16
30,000	2623.55	622.76	380.03	304.28	269.92	241.39
35,000	3060.81	726.55	443.37	355.00	314.91	281.62
40,000	3498.06	830.34	506.71	405.71	359.90	321.85
45,000	3935.32	934.13	570.05	456.42	404.88	362.09
50,000	4372.58	1037.92	633.38	507.14	449.87	402.32
55,000	4809.84	1141.71	696.72	557.85	494.85	442.55
60,000	5247.09	1245.51	760.06	608.56	539.84	482.78
65,000	5684.35	1349.30	823.40	659.28	584.83	523.01
70,000	6121.61	1453.09	886.74	709.99	629.81	563.24
75,000	6558.87	1556.88	950.07	760.70	674.80	603.47
80,000	6996.12	1660.67	1013.41	811.42	719.79	643.70

Look at the Monthly Amortization Table for 9%. Down the left are listed the amounts borrowed, followed by columns for each repayment period. Find the amount of the loan and then move to the amount next to it, for one year. A $20,000 loan to be repaid in one year requires a monthly payment of $1,749.03 (see table). The year's payments will be broken down as:

Month	Payment	Interest	Principal	Balance
				$20,000.00
1	$ 1,749.03	$150.00	$ 1,599.03	18,400.97
2	1,749.03	138.01	1,611.02	16,789.95
3	1,749.03	125.92	1,623.11	15,166.84
4	1,749.03	113.75	1,635.28	13,531.56
5	1,749.03	101.49	1,647.54	11,884.02
6	1,749.03	89.13	1,659.90	10,224.12
7	1,749.03	76.68	1,672.35	8,551.77
8	1,749.03	64.14	1,684.89	6,866.88
9	1,749.03	51.50	1,697.53	5,169.35
10	1,749.03	38.77	1,710.26	3,459.09
11	1,749.03	25.94	1,723.09	1,736.00
12	1,749.02*	13.02	1,736.00	–0–
Total	$20,988.35	$988.35	$20,000.00	

*Reduced for rounding

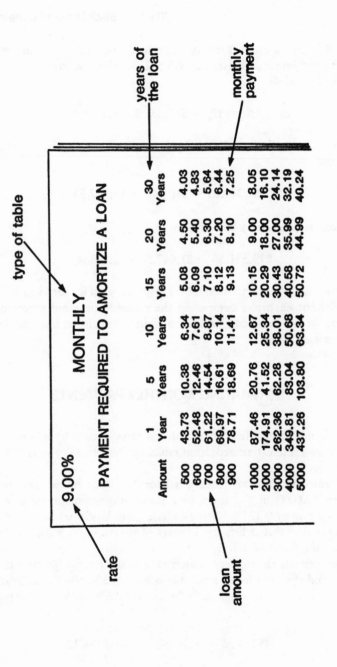

type of table

9.00% ← rate

MONTHLY

PAYMENT REQUIRED TO AMORTIZE A LOAN

years of the loan

monthly payment

Amount	1 Year	5 Years	10 Years	15 Years	20 Years	30 Years
500	43.73	10.38	6.34	5.08	4.50	4.03
600	52.48	12.46	7.61	6.09	5.40	4.83
700	61.22	14.54	8.87	7.10	6.30	5.64
800	69.97	16.61	10.14	8.12	7.20	6.44
900	78.71	18.69	11.41	9.13	8.10	7.25
1000	87.46	20.76	12.67	10.15	9.00	8.05
2000	174.91	41.52	25.34	20.29	18.00	16.10
3000	262.36	62.28	38.01	30.43	27.00	24.14
4000	349.81	83.04	50.68	40.58	35.99	32.19
5000	437.26	103.80	63.34	50.72	44.99	40.24

loan amount

Monthly interest is easily computed. For example, in the fifth month, the previous balance is $13,531.56. One-twelfth of 9% of that balance is $101.49.

$$(9\% \div 12) \times \$13,531.56 = \$101.49$$

This is subtracted from the total payment, and the remaining amount is principal:

$$\$1,749.03 - \$101.49 = \$1,647.54$$

The loan is reduced by that amount:

$$\$13,531.56 - \$1,647.54 = \$11,884.02$$

An interest amortization table is especially useful for loans of longer periods. For example, computing the monthly payment required for a 15-year or 30-year loan would be quite difficult without an interest amortization table.

ESTIMATING MONTHLY PAYMENTS

You will not always find actual interest rates quoted by a bank exactly listed on an interest amortization table. In these cases, you can estimate the required payment.

Example: You are adding a room to your house, and need to borrow $20,000 in the form of a home improvement loan. You are quoted a rate of 9.125%. You purchase a book of interest amortization tables, to find that it lists by quarters of percents—9, 9.25, 9.5, 9.75—but not in eighths of percents.

To estimate the payment required, find the average between the next higher and the next lower rates. On a loan of $20,000 for 10 years, the monthly payment at 9% is $253.36 and at 9.25%, $256.07. Average the two.

$$(\$253.36 + \$256.07) \div 2 = \$254.72$$

The same technique can be used to find a rate that is quoted in sixteenths of a percentage. For example, you are quoted a rate of 9.0625%.

Step 1: Calculate 9.125%, as above.

Step 2: Use next higher and next lower rates.

Payment at 9%	$253.36
Payment at 9.125%	$254.72

Step 3: Calculate the average.

$$(\$253.36 + \$254.72) \div 2 = \$254.04$$

Sometimes you need to calculate interest on a loan amount not found on the table. Most tables include rows for round amounts—$50, $100, $500, $1,000—but not for amounts in between.

Example: You are being given a 9% loan, payable over 10 years, in the amount of $21,550. Referring to the sample interest amortization table, add up the components of the total loan from the rows for $20,000, $1,000, $500, and $50:

	Loan Amount	Payment
	$20,000	$253.36
	1,000	12.67
	500	6.34
	50	.64
Total	$21,550	$273.01

REMAINING BALANCES

Most amortization table books contain two forms of tables: payment required to amortize a loan (described above) and remaining balance tables. With the first type of table, you know how much must be paid each month. By referring to a remaining balance table (see sample 9%

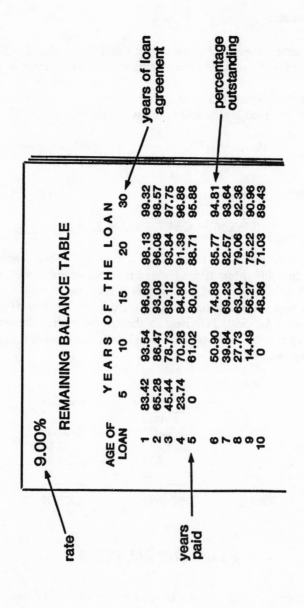

9.00% ← rate

REMAINING BALANCE TABLE

years of loan agreement →

percentage outstanding →

years paid ↑

AGE OF LOAN	YEARS OF THE LOAN				
	5	10	15	20	30
1	83.42	93.54	96.69	98.13	99.32
2	65.28	86.47	93.08	96.08	98.57
3	45.44	78.73	89.12	93.84	97.75
4	23.74	70.28	84.80	91.39	96.86
5	0	61.02	80.07	88.71	95.88
6		50.90	74.89	85.77	94.81
7		39.84	69.23	82.57	93.64
8		27.73	63.04	79.06	92.36
9		14.49	56.27	75.22	90.96
10		0	48.86	71.03	89.43

table), you will also be able to estimate the balance due at the end of each period. This table will show the following information:

1. The original term (length) of the loan, listed across the top row.
2. The age of the loan, listed in the far left-hand column.
3. The percentage rate for the table (with one table for each rate).
4. The percentage of the loan that will be outstanding at the end of each year, listed in each row.

Example: You have a second mortgage for $10,000, payable over 10 years at 9%. You would like to estimate the balance you will owe at the end of the fifth year.

Start by finding a 9% table. Go to the column showing an original term of 10 (years), then find the row for the age of loan of 5 (years). The percentage shown is 61.02. So the balance still due on the loan at that time will be:

$$\$10,000 \times 61.02\% = \$6,102.00$$

RATES OF AMORTIZATION

If you look at the remaining balance tables, some facts about loan amortization become evident.

1. The longer the term of the loan, the higher the interest cost.

2. The longer the term, the more slowly the loan balance decreases in the early years. For example, with a 30-year loan amortization at 9%, only one-half of the loan has been repaid in the 23rd year. The "Loan Payment Rate" graph shows the rate of payment on two loans, both for 9%. The 15-year term is paid down at a much faster rate than the 30-year loan. To compare the two, look again at the Remaining Balance Table. At the end of the tenth year, the 15-year loan is more than half paid; at the same point, 89.43% of the 30-year loan remains outstanding.

3. For only somewhat higher monthly payments, you can cut a long-term loan's period in half, and save a large amount of interest. To borrow $10,000 at 9%, you may have the choice of a 10- or 20-year

loan payment rate

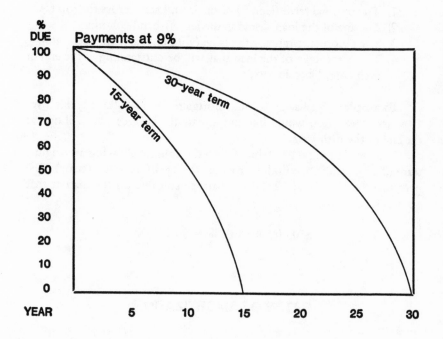

Payments at 9%

term. For a 10-year loan, the monthly payment would be $126.68, for a total interest expense of $5,201.60; to stretch the amortization over 20 years, you would have lower monthly payments—$89.98—but more than twice the interest: $11,595.20. So for an additional payment of $36.70 per month, the loan will be repaid in one-half the time, and at a savings of nearly $6,400.

These are crucial issues in budgeting a loan, in terms of the potential savings balanced against the effects on cash flow. Certainly, an additional $36.70 per month does not appear significant, and the benefits are attractive. However, when a greater amount of money is involved, the attractive savings may not be possible within the confines of cash flow.

Example: A company wants to borrow $500,000 and will pay 9%.

The term offered by a lender is 20 years, with a monthly payment of $1,799.46.

Paying the loan in 10 years instead of 20 would require monthly payments of $2,533.52, and would save the company $127,848 in interest. But the additional monthly payment of $734.06 would place too great a strain on cash flow, so the accelerated payment schedule is not taken.

As an alternative, the company may consider these choices:

1. Paying the loan over 15 years (monthly payment required: $2,028.54, and savings of $66,733 in total interest compared to the 20-year term).
2. Accepting the 20-year term, but later making additional payments to reduce the loan balance and save interest more rapidly (assuming the contract terms allow this).
3. Stay with the original, longer term, but make periodic payments against principal within the limits of available cash flow.

It may be possible to negotiate a lower rate when offering to pay back a loan in a shorter term, as the lender's risk period will not be as long. So the actual comparison may be between two different rates and periods. For example, a company desiring to borrow $500,000 may be offered the rate of 9% with a 20-year term. But the same lender may be willing to negotiate a loan for 15 years at 8.75%

The decision to accelerate a loan's payments should be made under the following guidelines:

1. The accelerated payment should be made from available cash reserves, so that future cash flow will not be adversely affected. For example, your company may have cash available during a high-volume season, but will need those reserves in slower months.

2. Acceleration should be undertaken only when the rate of interest is higher than the return on cash you are able to earn elsewhere. For example, if your loan rate is 9%, and you are able to earn only 7% elsewhere (in other investments or from putting profits back into expanded operations, for example), you will earn more by accelerating a loan. But if your return on cash is higher than your loan rate, you will do better to use available funds for outside investment or business purposes, and stay with the original loan term.

WORK PROJECT

1. Show the monthly payments due at 9% for the following loans (use the sample interest amortization table in this chapter).

   a. $5,000 for 20 years.   ....
   b. $10,000 for 5 years.   ....
   c. $12,350 for 10 years. ....

2. How much will you save in interest by paying a $5,000 loan in 5 years rather than 15, if the rate is 9%? _____

3. Calculate three months' payments, breaking down each payment between principal and interest and showing the balance at the end of each month, for a loan of $6,000 payable over 10 years at 9%.

_____

_____

_____

9

Present and Accumulated Value

"I'm astounded by people who want to know the universe when it's hard enough to find your way around Chinatown."

—Woody Allen

One harried manager was trying desperately to make sense out of the explanation in the front of a book of interest tables. Finally, in frustration, he called his bank and asked the loan officer for help. The banker asked, "Do you want to know the present value or the future worth?" After a confused pause, the manager answered, "Yes."

If you're frustrated when trying to figure out interest and amortization tables, relax. You're not alone. Most people are completely confused by the sheer number of tables to choose from and by the similarity of one to another. And, like trying to find your way around Chinatown, the instructions for using tables often only make matters worse.

Present value, future worth, or the amortization of 1 . . . the terminology alone is confusing, even if you don't look at a massive collection of columns and rows of eight-digit factors. But, if you take them one at a time, and start with a solid grounding in the purpose of each table, you can master this "secret art."

This chapter introduces the concepts of present and accumulated value, and will show you how to use computation tables. Each type of table will be explained completely, with examples. You probably already understand these values without necessarily using the terminology. For example, you know that if you deposit $100 per month for five years at 5% interest, it will grow to a sum of money. That's the *future worth* of your deposits, or the accumulated value. And if you want to save money over a period of time to end with $1,000, you know you have to deposit so much per month. The amount you have to deposit is the *present value* of that future amount, your target balance. Now it's just a matter of knowing how to quickly compute those factors, using interest tables.

The best way to overcome anxiety about an abstract mathematical idea is to master it. So this chapter will show you not only how to understand and use the tables, but also how to build a table of your own.

PURPOSES OF TABLES

In Chapters 7 and 8, some preliminary concepts of interest computation were introduced. Knowing how to compute interest and amortize a loan are important beginnings. But they're only part of the total story.

Example: You place money into a savings account where it will grow at interest for several years. Computing the future value is fairly straightforward when you are dealing with one initial deposit. But it becomes more complicated when you will be putting a sum of money away each month.

Example: You estimate that in five years, your child's college education will cost $7,200 per year. How much must you begin saving now so that you will have enough in each of the four years?

Example: You plan to buy a house in eight years, and want to accumulate $20,000 for a down payment. If you can earn 6% compounded monthly, what's the minimum you have to deposit starting now?

For these more complicated questions, you will need to refer to interest tables of one type or another. And that's where most of us run into trouble. Which table should you use? Even if you understand what you're trying to figure out, the terminology and explanations of tables are often more confusing than helpful. That's because there are six major tables for computing present or accumulated value, and each is subject to different methods of computing interest. To make matters worse, not every table is identified with the same name in every book of tables. The six tables are:

1. Accumulated Value of 1. *Other names:*

> Future Worth of 1
> Amount of 1
> Amount of 1 at Compound Interest
> Compound Amount of 1
> Amount of Annuity at 1

2. Accumulated Value of 1 per Period. *Other names:*

> Future Worth of 1 per Period
> Amount of 1 per Period
> Amount of 1 per Period at Compound Interest
> Compound Amount of 1 per Period
> Amount of Annuity at 1 per Period

3. Present Value of 1. *Other names:*

> Present Worth of 1
> Present Value Reversion of 1
> Present Value of 1 at Compound Interest

4. Sinking Fund Factors. *Other names:*

> Sinking Fund Payments
> Annuity Whose Accumulation at Compound Interest Is 1
> Periodic Payment of Annuity Whose Amount Is 1

5. Present Value of 1 per Period. *Other names:*

> Present Worth of 1 per Period
> Present Value of Ordinary Annuity 1 per Period
> Present Value of 1 per Period at Compound Interest

6. Amortization Payment. *Other names:*

> Partial Payment
> Partial Payment to Amortize 1
> Periodic Payment to Amortize 1
> Investment to Amortize 1
> Annuity Whose Present Value at Compound Interest Is 1
> Payment Required to Amortize a Loan

ACCUMULATED VALUE

Accumulated value is the future value of today's money, at a certain rate of interest, using a specific compounding method, for a given length of time.

Example: You place $100 in a savings account that pays 5% compounded annually. What will that be worth in three years?

Annual compounding is the easiest type. You simply multiply the amount on deposit by the annual rate. So the first year is the sum of $100 plus 5%, or $5.00. The second year's interest is 5% of $105, and the third year's interest is 5% of $110.25; see "Accumulated Value of 1" box.

So the accumulated value (also called "future worth") of $100 is $115.76 in this case. The specifics include annual compounding, a three-year term, and a single deposit of $100. A change in any of these specifics will result in a different accumulated value. For example, if the compounding is done quarterly instead of annually, the interest will be different. And if the term is longer, the accumulated value will be higher.

Accumulated Value of 1

This is an example of the computation identified on interest tables as "the accumulated value of 1." There is only one deposit, so the accumulated value is based on the growth of compound interest, not on additional deposits. This is the type of computation described in Chapter

7. It is not necessary, however, to do the calculations yourself; that's what the tables are for.

Accumulated Value of 1 per Period

If you deposit $100 at the beginning of *each* year, and interest is payable at the end of each year, the accumulated value will be different than for a single deposit (see "Accumulated Value" box). This is an example of what is called "the accumulated value of 1 per period." Interest is calculated based on the previous year's ending balance, since it is payable at the end of each year. Because a deposit is made each period, not just once, a different table must be used.

The reference to 1 is necessary in the interest of space. A table that showed the value factors for every possible amount of money would take up too much space, so you must multiply the 1 factor by the amount of money you have in mind. If you refer to a table showing the accumulated

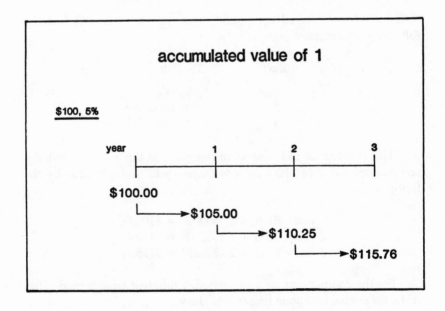

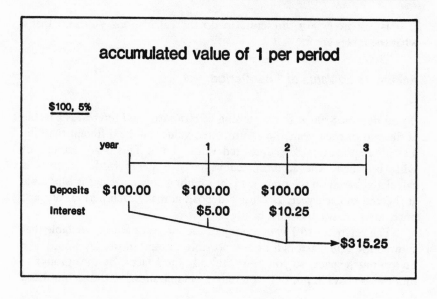

value of 1, with annual compounding of interest, you will find the following information:

Years	5% Rate
1	1.0500000
2	1.1025000
3	1.1576250

This is the value of 1, but we're concerned in this example with the accumulated value of $100. So it is necessary to multiply $100 by the factor on the table.

1 year: $100 × 1.0500000 = $105.00
2 years: $100 × 1.1025000 = $110.25
3 years: $100 × 1.1576250 = $115.76

For the computation of 1 per period, a different table is used. That table, for annual compounding at 5%, shows:

Years	5% Rate
1	1.0000000
2	2.0500000
3	3.1525000

The table reveals only the value of 1 per period, but the amount deposited is $100 per year. So the next step is to multiply $100 by the factor on the table:

$$1 \text{ year: } \$100 \times 1.0000000 = \$100.00$$
$$2 \text{ years: } \$100 \times 2.0500000 = \$205.00$$
$$3 \text{ years: } \$100 \times 3.1525000 = \$315.25$$

PRESENT VALUE

The opposite of accumulated value is present value. It is the value of money today, based on an amount you need in the future.

In three years you plan to attend your college reunion, which is taking place across the country. You estimate it will cost $1,000, and want to start saving now. You can earn 5% on your money, and can either put in a single sum of money (the present value of 1) or make periodic deposits (a sinking fund to create the target amount).

Present Value of 1

The Present Value of 1 table for 5% compounded annually shows that to accumulate 1 by the end of three years, you must deposit 0.8638375 today (see "Present Value of 1" box). Thus:

$$\$1,000 \times 0.8638375 = \$863.84$$

To prove this, figure out what you'll earn at 5%:

Year	Interest	Balance
		$ 863.84
1	$43.19	907.03
2	45.35	952.38
3	47.62	1,000.00

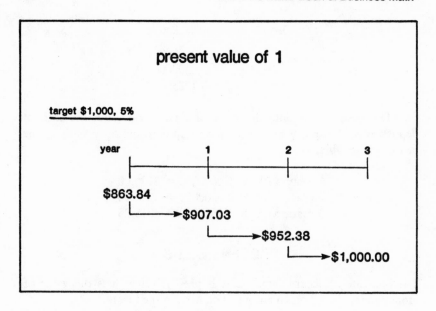

Sinking Fund Factors

To figure out how much you'll need to save if you prefer making yearly deposits, you must refer to the 5% annual compounding table for sinking fund factors. From this table you learn that the factor for three years is 0.3172085. So to accumulate $1,000 in three years, you will have to save $317.21 at the beginning of each year. See "Sinking Fund" box.

Year	Deposit	Interest	Balance
1	$317.21	$ 0	$ 317.21
2	317.21	15.86	650.28
3	317.21	32.51	1,000.00

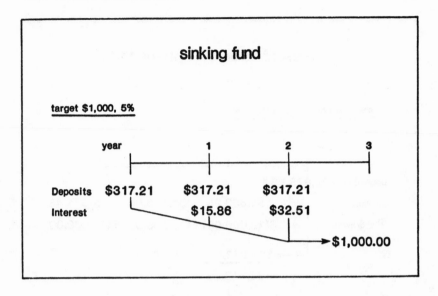

sinking fund

target $1,000, 5%

year	1	2	3

Deposits $317.21 $317.21 $317.21

Interest $15.86 $32.51

→ $1,000.00

Present Value of 1 per Period

A third type of present worth table shows what is required in periodic payments today to equal a series of future payments. For example, your company is leasing equipment on a three-year lease at a cost of $12,000 per year, for total payments of $36,000. You are instructed to deposit a sum of money today as a reserve to meet those payments. You can earn 5%, compounded annually. How much will you have to deposit now?

You start by referring to the Present Value of 1 per Period table. The factor for three years is 2.7232480. In order to have enough money available for payment of $12,000 per year, you need to deposit $32,678.98 today (see box):

$$\$12,000 \times 2.7232480 = \$32,678.98$$

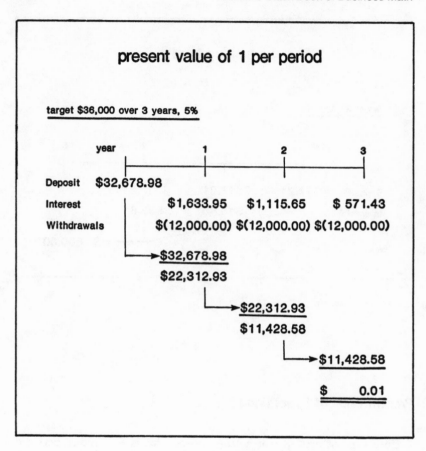

present value of 1 per period

target $36,000 over 3 years, 5%

year	1	2	3
Deposit	$32,678.98		
Interest	$1,633.95	$1,115.65	$ 571.43
Withdrawals	$(12,000.00)	$(12,000.00)	$(12,000.00)

$32,678.98
$22,312.93

$22,312.93
$11,428.58

$11,428.58

$ 0.01

To prove the calculation:

Year	Plus Interest	Less Withdrawal	Balance
			$32,678,98
1	$1,633.95	$12,000.00	22,312.93
2	1,115.65	12,000.00	11,428.58
3	571.43	12,000.00	.01

AMORTIZATION PAYMENTS

The final type of calculation involves figuring out how large a payment is required to pay off a loan over a specified period of years.

For example, to buy a car, you borrow $5,000 from a relative, agreeing to pay 8% compounded annually. In Chapter 8, examples were given of loan amortization tables that listed the dollar amounts of loans. Some tables are designed in this way, for ease of reference. But like other types of interest tables, these factors are often given for the "amortization of 1 per period." It is then necessary to multiply a table factor by the appropriate loan amount.

For the example of a $5,000 loan for three years, the 8% annual amortization table shows a factor of 0.3880335. Multiply the loan amount by the three-year factor to determine the annual payment required:

$$\$5,000 \times 0.3880335 = \$1,940.17$$

To prove this (see "Amortization Payments" box):

Year	Payment	Interest	Principal	Balance
				$5,000.00
1	$1,940.17	$400.00	$1,540.17	3,459.83
2	1,940.17	276.79	1,663.38	1,796.45
3	1,940.17	143.72	1,796.45	0

WHICH TABLE TO USE?

As with all applications of math, the job is much easier once you understand *why* a particular function is performed. In the case of amortization tables, you will better understand which one to use if you visualize the problem by creating a simple graph for yourself. We'll do it for six common situations.

1. You have $1,000 in the bank, and want to know what it will be worth in ten years. Your graph should show the single deposit and the number of periods (see Graph 1).

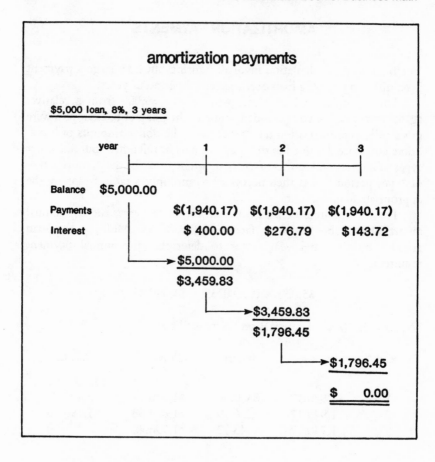

amortization payments

$5,000 loan, 8%, 3 years

year	1	2	3

Balance	$5,000.00			
Payments		$(1,940.17)	$(1,940.17)	$(1,940.17)
Interest		$ 400.00	$276.79	$143.72

$5,000.00
$3,459.83

$3,459.83
$1,796.45

$1,796.45

$ 0.00

From this, you can see that the single deposit will earn interest in each of the ten periods. So you should use the Accumulated Value of 1 table.

2. You plan to put $500 per year into a mutual fund. Based on past performance, you expect to earn 15% per year if you reinvest all

dividends. You are trying to estimate what the fund will be worth in five years (see Graph 2).

This is more complex than the first example. You must compute compound interest not only on one deposit, but on a series. This type of problem is solved by using the Accumulated Value of 1 per Period table; each period is a year.

3. You promise your 13-year-old son that you will give him $1,000 if he maintains a B average or better throughout his four years in high school. You need to know how much to put in a savings account today, earning a compound rate of 6.5%, to have $1,000 in four years. See Graph 3.

From your chart, you can see that this problem is the opposite of accumulated value. Refer to the Present Value of 1 table to decide what amount must be deposited now.

4. The terms of your mortgage call for a balloon payment (a lump sum) of $5,000, payable seven years from today. You want to put aside some money each year, enough so you'll have the cash when the payment is due (see Graph 4).

graph 1

$1,000   ?

.../ .../ .../ .../ .../ .../ .../ .../ .../ .../

YEAR   1   2   3   4   5   6   7   8   9   10

graph 2

$500 $500 $500 $500 $500   ?

... .../ ... .../ ... .../ ... .../ ... /

YEAR   1   2   3   4   5

graph 3

? $1,000

... .../ ... .../ ... .../ ... /

YEAR   1   2   3   4

To decide how much you will need to deposit each year, you must get a factor from the Sinking Fund Factors table.

5. You plan to retire in 30 years, at the age of 65. As a supplement to the profit-sharing plan at your company, you want to save enough each year (at 7% interest) to produce an additional $5,000 per year in retirement income for 20 years, until age 85. How much will you have to save over the next 30 years? See Graph 5.

You have 30 years to save, followed by 20 years during which you plan to withdraw $5,000 per year. To find the right factor, refer to the Accumulated Value of 1 per Period table.

6. You plan to buy your first house next year, and estimate your mortgage will be $85,000. With a repayment period of 15 years (or 180 months), you are quoted a rate of 10.25%. You must determine how much your monthly payments will be to amortize the loan (see Graph 6).

You know the total amount you're planning to borrow and the number of months or years in the term. To figure the monthly payment, refer to a Monthly Amortization Payment table.

graph 4

```
      ?   ?   ?   ?   ?   ?   ?  $5,000
      .../ .../ .../ .../ .../ .../ .../
YEAR    1   2   3   4   5   6   7
```

graph 5

```
          ?   ?           ?
YEAR    1 ... 2 ...      30 ... 31 ... 32 ...      50
                            $5,000  $5,000      $5,000
          SAVINGS PERIOD        RETIREMENT PERIOD
```

graph 6

```
          $85,000                        -0-
MONTH          ...1...2...3       ...............180
               ?  ?  ?                    ?
```

BUILD YOUR OWN TABLES

Knowing how to use a table may give you a degree of comfort. But to really master the concepts behind interest rate computations, learn how to construct a table on your own. This will give you an appreciation of the process in the calculation, taking the mystery out of it. It is also a helpful skill.

For example, you apply for a loan and are quoted the rate of 9.125%. But your tables give only quarter percentages—9% and 9.25%. You can estimate the amount as being somewhere between the two, or you can build a table on your own.

Below are step-by-step instructions for building all six tables, using 9% compounded annually in each case. Rounding is carried out to seven decimal places in all examples. For more comprehensive examples of all six types of interest tables, check your bookstore for one of these texts:

> *Compound Interest and Annuity Tables,* McGraw-Hill, $5.95.
> *Comprehensive Compound Interest Tables,* Contemporary Books, $4.95.
> *Interest Amortization Tables,* McGraw-Hill, $4.95.
> *Loan Payment Tables,* Contemporary Books, $6.95.
> *Monthly Interest Amortization Tables,* Contemporary Books, $4.95.
> *Monthly Payments,* Barron's, $4.95.

Accumulated Value of 1

Purpose: To compute the future value of $1 with interest payable at the beginning of each period.

Step 1: Add 1 to the interest rate in decimal form:

$$1 + .09 = 1.09$$

Step 2: Extend this rate to compute the factor for the first year:

$$1.09 = 1.0900000$$

Step 3: Multiply each previous year's factor by 1.09:

$$2\text{nd year: } 1.09 \times 1.0900000 = 1.1881000$$
$$3\text{rd year: } 1.09 \times 1.1881000 = 1.2950290$$
$$4\text{th year: } 1.09 \times 1.2950290 = 1.4115816$$

Your table:

Year	9% Rate
1	1.0900000
2	1.1881000
3	1.2950290
4	1.4115816

Accumulated Value of 1 per Period

Purpose: To compute the future value of $1 per period with interest payable at the end of each period.

Step 1: The first year's factor is always 1.

Step 2: Each subsequent year is computed by multiplying the previous year's factor by 1.09, and adding 1.

$$2\text{nd year: } (1.0000000 \times 1.09) + 1 = 2.0900000$$
$$3\text{rd year: } (2.0900000 \times 1.09) + 1 = 3.2781000$$
$$4\text{th year: } (3.2781000 \times 1.09) + 1 = 4.5731290$$

Your table:

Year	9% Rate
1	1.0000000
2	2.0900000
3	3.2781000
4	4.5731290

Present Value of 1

Purpose: To compute the amount of deposit required today to accumulate a target amount in the future, with interest payable at the end of each period.

Step 1: For the first year, divide 1 by 1.09:

$$1 \div 1.09 = 0.9174311$$

Step 2: For subsequent periods, divide the previous factor by 1.09:

2nd year: $0.9174311 \div 1.09 = 0.8416799$
3rd year: $0.8416799 \div 1.09 = 0.7721834$
4th year: $0.7721834 \div 1.09 = 0.7084251$

Your table:

Year	9 % Rate
1	0.9174311
2	0.8416799
3	0.7721834
4	0.7084251

Sinking Fund Payments

Purpose: To compute the amount of deposits required per period to accumulate a target amount in the future, with interest payable at the end of each period.

Step 1: Divide 1 by the factor on the Accumulated Value of 1 per Period table to compute each sinking fund factor.

1st year: $1 \div 1.0000000 = 1.0000000$
2nd year: $1 \div 2.0900000 = 0.4784688$
3rd year: $1 \div 3.2781000 = 0.3050547$
4th year: $1 \div 4.5731290 = 0.2186686$

Your table:

Year	9% Rate
1	1.0000000
2	1.4784688
3	0.3050547
4	0.2186686

Present Value of 1 per Period

Purpose: To determine the amount of deposit required today to meet future periodic payments, with interest payable at the end of each period.

Step 1: Refer to the Present Value of 1 table.

Step 2: For each period, add the accumulated factors on the table:

Year	Present Value of 1	Present Value of 1 per period
1	0.9174311	0.9174311
2	0.8416799	1.7591110
3	0.7721834	2.5312944
4	0.7084251	3.2397195

Your table:

Year	9% Rate
1	0.9174311
2	1.7591110
3	2.5312944
4	3.2397195

Amortization Payments

Purpose: To compute the amount of periodic payments required to amortize a loan within a specified number of periods, with interest payable at the end of each period.

Step 1: Refer to the Present Value of 1 per Period table.

Step 2: For each period, divide 1 by the factor on the Present Value of 1 per Period table:

$$1\text{st year:} \quad 1 \div 0.9174311 = 1.0900000$$
$$2\text{nd year:} \quad 1 \div 1.7591110 = 0.5684689$$
$$3\text{rd year:} \quad 1 \div 2.5312944 = 0.3950547$$
$$4\text{th year:} \quad 1 \div 3.2397195 = 0.3086686$$

Your table:

Year	9% Rate
1	1.0900000
2	0.5684689
3	0.3950547
4	0.3086686

WORK PROJECT

1. Build a table for the first five years, showing the accumulated value of 1 for 6.25%.

_____

_____

_____

_____

_____

2. Use the table below to answer the following:

Sinking Fund Factors, Annual, 7%

Year	Factor
1	1.0000000
2	0.4830917
3	0.3110516
4	0.2252281
5	0.1738906

a. How much must be deposited each year at 7% to accumulate a fund of $1,000 in five years? ....
b. Prove the accuracy of this table by working out the compound interest for five years.

_____

_____

_____

_____

_____

3. Below are amortization payments for 8.5%, compounded monthly. Use this to answer the questions.

Amortization Payments, Monthly, 8.5%

Year	Factor
5	0.0205165
10	0.0123985
15	0.0098473
20	0.0086782
25	0.0080522
30	0.0076891

What is the required monthly payment for the following loans, based on 8.5% and monthly compounding?

a. $32,850 for 15 years.   ....
b. $50,000 for 25 years.   ....
c. $5,333 for 5 years.   ....
d. $85,000 for 30 years.   ....

10

Rates of Return

"A billion here, a billion there . . . pretty soon, it adds up to real money."

—Senator Everett Dirksen

Results for ten months were reported by the treasurer at a financial review meeting of a small corporation. Debts were down, cash flow was healthy, and sales were on the rise. One executive expressed concern about the amount of federal taxes that would be due on unexpected profits. The treasurer responded, "If we put forth an effort, we might still have time to generate a small operating loss."

What rate of return did your company make last year? That depends. Are you calculating your answer based on sales, net worth, or earnings per share? A profit, by itself, doesn't always tell the whole story—especially if the company is barely holding onto its market share. A net loss for the year doesn't necessarily mean the end is in sight. Losses sometimes occur because the company is investing to develop new markets.

There are a number of ways to calculate return. And return by itself, like other statistical information, is meaningless until it is compared and put into perspective.

Investment returns are always stated as a percentage of the amount invested. For example, you purchase 100 shares of a company's stock for $27 per share and sell it at $31—a profit of $4 per share, or 14.8% return. When a corporation reports, however, profits can be characterized in different ways:

1. Net profits as a percentage of gross sales.
2. Net profits as a percentage of equity.
3. Net profits as a percentage increase over the previous year.
4. Earnings per share or an increase in earnings per share over prior periods.
5. Pretax profits or aftertax profits, as a percentage of gross sales or equity.

So when a company states, "We earned an 8% profit last year," it can mean a number of different results. When corporations report profits, they often emphasize the change more than the rate. For example, one company reported a dismal 1.3% of sales going to the bottom line. But . . . that represented a 175% improvement over the previous year, so that was the emphasis in the annual report.

INVESTMENT RETURN

To further confuse the question, terms used for investment return (or yield) are often different from those used to describe corporate profits. For example, your company has invested some of its cash in a savings account, with an interest rate of 5.5% per year. This is known as the *nominal yield*. The *annual yield*, though, is different: Because interest is compounded monthly, the annual comes out to 5.64%.

Another result, *current yield*, applies when the value of your investment changes. For example, your company buys a $1,000 bond that pays interest at the nominal yield of 8%. But a year later, that same bond is valued at a premium of 108 (meaning that for each $1,000 invested, the current market value is $1,080). The current yield is the nominal yield divided by today's market value. You are receiving $80 per year (8% of the face value of the bond), but current value is $1,080. Current yield is 7.41% ($80 ÷ $1,080).

So you can talk about nominal, annual, and current yield, and all three are different. But there's still more. When you finally sell your investment, you will get the *net yield*, which is the combination of earnings from interest or dividends, plus capital gains (the difference between what you paid for the investment and what you sold it for). For example, you buy shares of stock for $4,200. When you sell 13 months later, you receive $4,850. But while you held the stock, you also received $180 in dividends. Your total profit is:

Capital gain	$650
Dividends	180
Total profit	$830

Your net yield, based on the amount you invested, is 19.8% ($830 ÷ $4,200).

If you want to express the net yield on an annual basis, you'll have to make another adjustment. In this example, the stock was held for 13 months. So the *annual net yield* will be 12/13 of this total:

$$12/13 \times 19.8\% = 18.28\%$$

If you had held the stock for only six months, the annual net yield would be 39.6%, or twice 19.8%, since six months represents only half a full year.

A final type of return used by investors is the *aftertax yield*. That's what you have left over after computing the portion you owe in taxes. For example, on an annual net yield of 18.28%, you are liable for taxes at the marginal rate of 15%. So your aftertax yield is only 85% of the computed amount:

$$18.28\% \times 85\% = 15.54\%$$

For a quick summary of all these various returns, see "Types of Investment Yield."

Types of Investment Yield

Nominal yield is the stated amount, before compounding is computed. Example: a savings account pays a nominal yield of 6%.

Annual yield is the actual rate earned after compounding. If that 6% account is compounded monthly, the annual yield is 6.17%.

Current yield is the rate based on today's value. A bond may carry a current market value above or below your purchase price; thus, the current yield will vary with market value.

Net yield is total return on an investment, including capital gains and earnings.

Annual net yield is an adjustment of net yield to reflect a 12-month holding period.

Aftertax yield is the rate earned in one year, minus the percentage that goes to taxes.

BUSINESS RETURNS

Just as investment yield can mean any number of different types of return, business returns can also be computed in a number of ways. The most common expression of "return" in business is the *net profit rate*. On sales of $10 million net profit was $1 million or 10%. But what does that mean? Is it pretax or aftertax? Are there any one-time adjustments on the books that distort the rate for purposes of comparison?

Terminology varies from one company to another, but as a general rule, the following definitions are used:

Net operating profit. The amount of profit earned from operations, but before federal income taxes are taken into account.

Aftertax profit. Profits after estimating the liability for federal income taxes.

Net profit margin. The percentage that net profits are, compared to sales. It should be made clear whether the "net profit margin" is reported on the basis of net operating profit or aftertax profit. Some companies separate some types of income and expenses from the reported net operating profit number. They may list "other income," including interest income, foreign exchange gains, discounts received, and capital gains; and "other expenses," including interest expense, foreign exchange losses, discounts granted, and capital losses.

When this occurs, and depending upon the amount of "other" income or loss, reporting of net profits will not always be accurate. For example, a company may report that its net operating profit was 13% of sales. But that same company may be depending heavily on outside financing, and have a large interest expense each year. If that is included *below* the operating profit line on a financial statement, it means it was broken out from the total, and actual net will be considerably lower.

In a comparison between two different companies, between your company and an assumed norm, or between one year and the next, the treatment of "other" income and expenses, consideration for taxes, and other inconsistencies must be brought into the picture. Depending on adjustments that may have occurred during the year, a reported net profit might not reflect a true picture.

Example: Your company is considering expanding and offering a new line of business. To forecast the sales volume and profit level that might be expected, you analyze the latest financial statement of a competitor who is also involved in that business (that company is publicly traded, so its financial information is available to anyone). It reported a net operating profit of 8.2% last year:

Gross sales	$86,534,600
Cost of goods sold	47,703,200
Gross profit	$38,831,400
Operating expenses	31,735,500
Net operating profit	$ 7,095,900

But before you judge that rate, look through the report for other factors that should be considered. You find two significant points:

1. An adjustment was made to the books to reflect a change in inventory valuation method. This created a one-time profit adjustment of $2,700,000. When this is taken away from profits as reported, it leaves only $4,395,900, or 5.1%.

2. The profits as reported show no allowance for federal income taxes. This is because the corporation has carryover losses this year, which will cancel out its tax liability. However, this will not repeat next year. Their tax rate is 15%. With the one-time inventory adjustment in mind, tax on an adjusted profit of $4,395,900 would have been $659,385, reducing profits to $3,736,515, or 4.3% of gross sales. A company's profits may contain one-time, or "extraordinary," items for several reasons—inventory valuation changes, profit or loss from foreign exchange rates, sale or abandonment of a large amount of inventory or a

major capital asset, or the payment or receipt of funds resulting from litigation. In comparing and computing profits based on sales, these adjustments should first be removed from the total profit. And, of course, the reported amount should be net of any taxes due. In cases where the company is not liable for taxes because of carryover losses, you should still make an allowance for the amount that would be due, to make a year-to-year comparison valid.

In practice, reports of net profit are not adjusted for exceptions arising from extraordinary items or tax loss carryovers. These issues are explained in footnotes or left for the reader to interpret.

THE TIME FACTOR

There are important distinctions between investment and business returns, as we have seen. But there is one more factor that must be taken into consideration to qualify the real significance of a return: How long did it take to earn it?

For example, you put $1,000 into a mutual fund. Three years later, it has grown to $1,450. That's a total return of 45%. But, since it took three years, it averages out to only 15% per year.

The same qualifier must be applied to business. For example, a new corporation earns 3.4% during its first reporting period (aftertax net). But that period only lasted five months. On an annualized basis (the equivalent return for a full year), the percentage of return was 8.2%:

$$12/5 \times 3.4\% = 8.2\%$$

Time must be used to adjust total return, in addition to the other factors.

ANALYZING RETURNS: THEORY APPLIED

Four years ago, your company invested $150,000 to develop a new division. You have been assigned to report on the profitability of that investment.

Intent on judging the profitability of that decision, management decided that separate records should be maintained. Profits and losses during the last four years were:

First year	$23,500
Second year	(8,400)
Third year	(4,400)
Fourth year	6,500
Total	$17,200

The question is, has the return on this investment been worthwhile? You begin by computing your company's average after-tax return for the same period. You use the following information:

Year	Gross Sales	Net Profit	Average Equity
1	$12.7 million	$ 742,800	$38.4 million
2	16.4 million	1,064,500	42.6 million
3	19.8 million	1,315,800	44.3 million
4	21.6 million	1,492,300	47.7 million

From this information, you compute the following ratios (see Chapter 4):

Year	Net Return	Return on Equity
1	5.8%	1.9%
2	6.5	2.5
3	6.6	3.0
4	6.9	3.1

To compare, the $150,000 investment in the new division yielded $17,200 in four years, or a total of 11.5%. That averages out to 2.9% per year. That's higher than the average return on equity, but lower than the net return. What conclusions can you draw from this? First, you must address these questions:

1. If the $150,000 had been available for other purposes, would it have increased sales at a rate higher than the division earned?

2. What is the outlook for future profit levels in the division, compared to prospects for your company as a whole?
3. Is there a buyer for the division?

If that $150,000 had been used to promote the primary line of business, the company could have received a higher return on its money, if it maintained the consistent pattern of growth in net return. But you must also consider whether the sales levels reached were the maximum possible, regardless of capital available. It may be that the company can capture only so much of its possible market, with competitors and customer buying limits in mind.

You must also consider the division's potential for future profits when analyzing the profitability of the investment. It is doubtful that your company had only the four-year term in mind when it made the decision to invest.

Your company might consider selling the new division to an outside buyer. Two questions must be asked: Is an interested buyer available? What is the market value of the investment?

Since you probably don't know all the answers to these questions, your report should include the analysis and mention these points. This allows management to draw conclusions with as much information as possible.

There may be other points that make a purely financial analysis invalid. For example, the investment might have been made in order to acquire land and buildings, whose current market value is much higher than book value, a factor not reflected in net profits. Or the investment might have been to eliminate a competitor. In that case, the benefit comes in the form of a higher market share and, possibly, a higher rate of return for your company—again, a benefit not shown in the division's net results.

The point here is that the question of return is not a simple one. You cannot simply compare one year to the next, or one company to another. Accurate analysis will depend on:

1. The method of comparison (to net return or return on investment).

2. The time factor (number of years required to produce the return, and what that means on an annualized basis).
3. The future potential for increased earnings and return (an investment may be about to pay off, for example).
4. The realistic potential for return from operating capital (could your company have increased sales and profits if the money had been available?).
5. Adjustment for one-time extraordinary items.
6. Nonfinancial benefits, such as the market value of assets that may exceed book value.
7. The significance of return when compared to other indicators of financial strength, such as the trend in working capital, debt and equity, and sales volume.

As you can see, when you're asked to summarize the return on an investment, the request may lead to more questions than it answers. But there is a solution.

You probably do not have all the information available to draw correct conclusions in reporting return. That's because the future potential for profits is always a major factor in deciding whether an investment is viable, whether it's a new division, cash placed into an interest-bearing account, or the value of company stock.

The solution is to prepare your reports to supply as much information as possible, so that management can use what it considers valid. This is preferable to drawing a conclusion based on a set of assumptions, only to be told that your assumptions are incorrect.

For example, you are to prepare a report on the profitability of a subsidiary in which your company has invested capital. You should include:

1. Net return (profits compared to sales) for each year, both before and after federal taxes.
2. Net return for the total period being studied, on a before- and aftertax basis.
3. Return on investment each year.
4. Return on investment for the entire period.

WORK PROJECT

1. Your company has invested $8,000 in a savings account that pays 6.25%, compounded quarterly.

   a. What is the nominal yield? ....
   b. What is the annual yield, considering that interest is compounded quarterly (see Chapter 7)? ....

2. In its portfolio of marketable securities, your company has a $1,000 bond that yields 8%. It is currently valued at 104 ($1,040 for each $1,000 invested). What is the current yield? ....

3. You are reviewing the annual report of a company that reports $825,400 profits on sales of $9.63 million, or 8.57%. But in footnotes to the statement, you find a one-time adjustment for foreign exchange rates of $32,000 included in profits. Also, the company carried over a loss from the previous year, saving $122,000 in federal income taxes. Without these adjustments, what would the net return have been?

11

Calculations for Your Career

The CEO of a very large corporation was being interviewed by a reporter. "I realized many years ago that there is a secret to success," he revealed. "When I began my career, I set the goal that I'd save my company more money than it cost them to keep me on the payroll."

"So is that how you rose to become the controlling stockholder of a major company?"

"Yes. And if I hadn't come to that realization early on in my career, I would have had to make my money the old-fashioned way—by inheriting it."

As an employee, you will be judged in one of two ways. Either you are part of the cost of doing business, or a resource for the creation of profits. The way you'll be perceived by your boss and by top management depends on your own point of view. If you think that your job includes the responsibility for coming up with money-saving ideas, and you approach others with that motive in mind, then you have discovered the secret.

Example: After a company was taken over by another corporation, the work load in the word processing and typing section rose dramatically. More reports were required, more frequently. The supervisor reviewed time cards for the period since the change in ownership. Overtime was on the rise, and she expected more increases in the near future. Her conclusion: It was time to hire an additional employee. But her supervisor turned down the idea; the new management had placed a freeze on hiring.

Then the supervisor took a different approach. She summarized the cost of overtime, demonstrating how a new employee would save money. She wrote:

An idea to reduce expenses:
The 14 employees in the word processing and typing section earn an average of $9.12 per hour. But overtime in the department, which costs 1.5 times the hourly rate, has been increasing in recent weeks, and is expected to continue growing at present staff levels.
A summary of the last seven weeks:

Week Ending	Overtime Hours
4/18	36
4/23	42
4/30	27
5/7	67
5/14	46
5/21	83
5/28	78

The cost of overtime during the latest week was greater than $1,000. Based on current work load and projects scheduled for the next two months, this trend will continue.
Recommendation: Hire one additional employee now at the rate of $9.12 per hour (estimate). The work a new employee will perform will reduce department payroll costs by approximately $175 per week.

The report was reviewed and sent on to the new management, and the idea was approved. The proposal was summarized logically, and the argument was supported with facts. This makes the case indisputable.

There's only one smart move management could make in response: to take advantage of the opportunity. The return on the investment is too good to pass up.

The difference made by a good report? If you ask your supervisor to solve your problem, you invariably are suggesting spending more money. But if you point out a problem and propose a profitable solution to it, then you are a valuable adviser.

EVERYTHING IS AN INVESTMENT

Think about your job from an investor's point of view. As a stockholder in a corporation, you want profits to rise, to increase the value of your stock and hence the value of your investment. From an executive's point of view, the same argument can be made. It is management's task to do its best for the stockholders. And part of the job is to constantly keep one eye on profits.

When you use this orientation, every decision becomes an investment decision. Hiring new employees is an added expense, so that means lower profits—unless the investment in a new employee reduces other expenses and, as a result, adds more to the bottom line. Putting money into advertising, paying travel expenses for employees, or buying typewriters and desks are all forms of investment, and they either increase profits or drain them.

Whenever you ask for something—an increase in staff, a raise in pay, a new desk—take the approach that, from your supervisor's point of view, everything is an investment. If you're able to track the cost factors, you will not only improve your value as an employee, you'll probably get what you want more often. Let's look at two ways of handling common office situations.

1. You are proposing a 15% increase in pay for an employee in your department.

Argument 1
She's been doing a pretty good job and gets along with other people in the department. And we gave another employee 15% last month.

Argument 2

This employee came up with an idea that is saving the company more than $2,000 per month. Her insights and leadership make her a valuable asset that we can't afford to lose to another company.

2. You want the company to buy a new typewriter for your department.

Argument 1

You bought a new typewriter for another department. Why do we have to use this older model?

Argument 2

The typewriter we're using has broken down three times in the last two months. The total cost of these breakdowns has been $376 ($318 for repairs and $58 for idle employee time), plus the intangible cost of delays in work completion. Historically, the repair cost of typewriters older than five years increases 14% in the sixth year and 38% in the seventh year. Recommendation: Replace this machine with a new model costing $1,114. This will yield a profit in less than three years in repair bills alone, based on the company's historical average.

The second argument in each case depends on fact, rather than the less relevant—but more common—bases on which companies are asked to spend (or invest) money.

MOVING AVERAGES

Whenever you request that the company spend more money, you will get better responses if you approach the question from the investor's point of view. The same argument applies when you're reporting and summarizing information.

Example: The president of your company has questioned whether the level of travel and entertainment is justified. The marketing vice president argues that the expense is necessary to generate a higher volume of new orders, but the president isn't convinced. You are given the assignment of summarizing travel and entertainment expenses in comparison to the level of new orders placed, by month.

You gather this information for the last two years:

Month	Travel and Entertainment	New Orders Placed
Jan	$14,360	15,255
Feb	9,411	11,562
Mar	22,505	8,445
Apr	18,003	21,788
May	6,542	17,692
Jun	20,045	4,417
Jul	31,490	6,003
Aug	14,348	14,539
Sep	7,562	22,031
Oct	11,206	11,832
Nov	22,605	10,043
Dec	20,303	16,828
Jan	$14,936	15,411
Feb	8,230	17,392
Mar	31,499	22,831
Apr	18,393	18,439
May	6,395	19,944
Jun	11,171	18,636
Jul	9,749	12,868
Aug	10,522	19,800
Sep	8,498	14,230
Oct	16,449	23,063
Nov	34,500	19,945
Dec	23,478	17,440

There are several problems with this information, as far as your report is concerned:

1. There is no consistency on a monthly basis, and no absolute seasonal tendency.

2. Orders are booked as they're placed, but travel and entertainment paid during the month may well apply to a previous period.

3. The summary, by itself, does not enable someone reading your report to determine whether the travel and entertainment investment is justified by the level of new orders. Even placing the information on a chart will produce no absolute conclusion about the validity of information. A mere summary of facts isn't enough; you must be able to provide more than history, so that questions may be answered.

For this type of information, the moving average is the best reporting method. With this technique, you drop off the oldest factor as you progress through the range. For example, a 12-month average will be based on February through January (for the following January), then March through February (for the following February). So for any given month, the range on which the moving average is based is made up of the current month and the previous 11 months.

To compute the moving average for the last year:

Step 1. Add the results from February of the first year through January of the second year.

Travel and entertainment = $198,956

Step 2. Subtract the February total from your first range, and add the second year's factor for February.

$198,956 − $9,411 + $8,230 = $197,775

Step 3. For each subsequent month, drop off the oldest and add the most recent to develop a new range.

Step 4. When you have completed the twelfth month, check the accuracy of your range by adding the last 12 factors. Make sure this agrees with the total computed in steps 1 through 3.

Step 5. Divide each range by 12 to determine the 12-month moving average.

Applying this technique to the historical information on travel and entertainment and orders placed:

Month	Travel and Entertainment		New Orders Placed	
	12 Months	Average	12 Months	Average
Jan	$198,956	16,580	160,591	13,383
Feb	197,775	16,481	166,421	13,868
Mar	206,769	17,231	180,807	15,067
Apr	207,159	17,263	177,458	14,788
May	207,012	17,251	179,710	14,976
Jun	198,138	16,512	193,929	16,161
Jul	176,397	14,700	200,794	16,733
Aug	172,571	14,381	206,055	17,171
Sep	173,507	14,459	198,254	16,521
Oct	178,750	14,896	209,485	17,457
Nov	190,645	15,887	219,387	18,282
Dec	193,820	16,152	219,999	18,333

Moving averages should definitely be expressed on a graph. Because the significance of month-to-month changes is absorbed in the average, the trend is best expressed visually. The chart showing 12-month moving average is an example of a two-scale line graph. The top line is the 12-month moving average in orders placed, using the scale at the left; and the lower line is for travel and entertainment, using the scale at the right.

When drawing conclusions from a moving average, you must speak in generalized terms and qualify any conclusions you reach. So an accompanying narrative to a graph like this one could read:

> The increase in orders placed during the last year was compared to the level of travel and entertainment expenses for the same period. The graph reflects a 12-month moving average of each.
>
> The positive trend in the average orders placed per month is greater than the increase in the moving average of travel and entertainment expenses, which supports the contention that this expense is justified.
>
> This conclusion does not take into consideration other relevant factors, such as the effect on new orders of advertising, market conditions or competition, or changes in the company's field sales force.

12-month moving average

Comparison:
orders placed to travel & entertainment expense

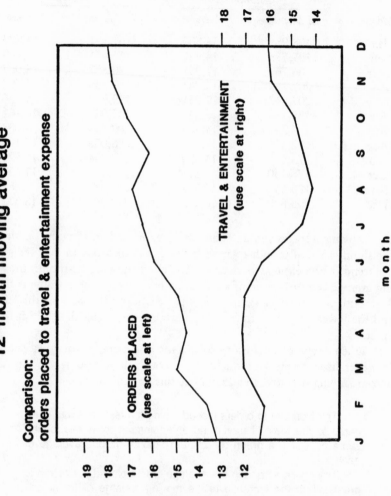

average: thousands of dollars

ORDERS PLACED
(use scale at left)

TRAVEL & ENTERTAINMENT
(use scale at right)

month

average: thousands of orders

The Relevance of Math

From the example above, it should be apparent that the whole story is rarely confined to the numbers. Imagine how these results are distorted if advertising budgets tripled during the year; if the company's sales force doubled; if a major competitor went out of business; or a new product line opened entirely new markets for your company.

A comprehensive analysis would have to bring those major points into the report, if known. But still, there's a problem. You were asked to prepare a comparison of two factors: travel and entertainment expenses and new orders placed. Is it proper to complicate the analysis with other points? It is if those other factors will alter the conclusion that can and should be drawn.

Some realities, though, to keep in mind:

1. There may be a short deadline on completion of the report, making it impossible for you to perform the detailed analysis required. That's why it's a smart idea to qualify any conclusions by mentioning other factors.

2. The motive for requesting the report may be something other than the desire for the whole story. For example, an executive requests a report as a way to defend excessive travel and entertainment expenses. You'll have to wrestle with the moral dilemma involved.

3. As we've already seen, a comparison such as this is far from objective. The numbers don't tell the whole story, even when reduced to a moving average. The results will be affected by changes in marketing strategy, the mix of field salespeople, and the nature of competition and the market. Those points cannot be reduced to a graph, and will not be clarified by a moving average.

In other words, the real significance of information prepared with financial history is never black and white. There are limits to the usefulness of math as a medium for reporting. What's required is the combination of skill in the efficient expression of numbers, added to your ability to interpret and qualify what those numbers reveal.

It's the balance between analysis of pure information—the black and white—and the less tangible insights you gain from experience—the gray areas—that ultimately convert more data into valuable and useful solutions. And that, from the company's point of view, makes you a valuable and useful employee, one who more than justifies the investment in you.

WORK PROJECT

1. You propose replacing a photocopy machine with a more powerful model. What information should you include to support your idea?

_____

_____

_____

2. Sales levels for the past 14 months were:

Nov	$743,650	Jun	$910,005
Dec	710,054	Jul	980,406
Jan	714,371	Aug	981,115
Feb	800,340	Sep	930,640
Mar	788,404	Oct	841,703
Apr	849,933	Nov	806,335
May	882,600	Dec	773,540

Compute a three-month moving average for the January–December period.

_____

_____

_____

_____

3. Using the same information in Question 2, what other factors should be considered in your analysis of the trend in sales?

_____

_____

_____

_____

Appendix

Work Project Answers

CHAPTER 1

1. This is a multiple-part problem and must take into account each of the assumptions you are given. First is the assumption that last year's sales level of $91,200 per person (or $7,600 per month) will increase by 1.5% per month:

$$1.5\% \times \$7,600 = \$114$$

Adding this amount to production throughout the year results in:

Month	Volume	Month	Volume
Jan	$7,714	Jul	$8,398
Feb	7,828	Aug	8,512
Mar	7,942	Sep	8,626
Apr	8,056	Oct	8,740
May	8,170	Nov	8,854
Jun	8,284	Dec	8,968

Production by new recruits to be forecast on the basis of one-half of last year's average production level. That was $7,600, and 50% is $3,800. It is also assumed that this production will not be booked until three months after hire date.

The assumption for the number of recruits is done in two parts. The existing sales force will decline by an average of three people per month.

New recruits will average four per month and 50% are expected to leave six months later.

	Existing Force				New Recruits		
Month	Start	Less	Number	Start	Plus	Less	Number
Jan	366	3	363	0	4		4
Feb	363	3	360	4	4		8
Mar	360	3	357	8	4		12
Apr	357	3	354	12	4		16
May	354	3	351	16	4		20
Jun	351	3	348	20	4		24
Jul	348	3	345	24	4	2	26
Aug	345	3	342	26	4	2	28
Sep	342	3	339	28	4	2	30
Oct	339	3	336	30	4	2	32
Nov	336	3	333	32	4	2	34
Dec	333	3	330	34	4	2	36

The next step is to compute volume by multiplying the production assumption by the number of people estimated to be with the company.

A. Existing sales force

Month	Average Production	Existing Sales Force	Total Volume ($000)
Jan	$7,714	363	$ 2,800.2
Feb	7,828	360	2,818.1
Mar	7,942	357	2,835.3
Apr	8,056	354	2,851.8
May	8,170	351	2,867.7
Jun	8,284	348	2,882.8
Jul	8,398	345	2,897.3
Aug	8,512	342	2,911.1
Sep	8,626	339	2,924.2
Oct	8,740	336	2,936.6
Nov	8,854	333	2,948.4
Dec	8,968	330	2,959.4
		Total	$34,632.9

B. New recruits

Month	Average Production	New Recruits	Total Volume ($000)
Jan	$3,800	0*	$ 0
Feb	3,800	0	0
Mar	3,800	0	0
Apr	3,800	4	15.2
May	3,800	8	30.4
Jun	3,800	12	45.6
Jul	3,800	16	60.8
Aug	3,800	20	76.0
Sep	3,800	24	91.2
Oct	3,800	26	98.8
Nov	3,800	28	106.4
Dec	3,800	30	114.0
Total			$ 638.4

*3-month delay

To summarize your forecast, combine the projected total volume for existing sales force and new recruits.

Month	Existing Sales Force	New Recruits	Total Volume ($000)
Jan	$ 2,800.2	$ 0	$ 2,800.2
Feb	2,818.1	0	2,818.1
Mar	2,835.3	0	2,835.3
Apr	2,851.8	15.2	2,867.0
May	2,867.7	30.4	2,898.1
Jun	2,882.8	45.6	2,928.4
Jul	2,897.3	60.8	2,958.1
Aug	2,911.1	76.0	2,987.1
Sep	2,924.2	91.2	3,015.4
Oct	2,936.6	98.8	3,035.4
Nov	2,948.4	106.4	3,054.8
Dec	2,959.4	114.0	3,073.4
Total	$34,632.9	$ 638.4	$35,271.3

2. To amend the projection, start with the final figures from the previous answers. The seasonal slowdown will take place during the last four months only, and the slight increase in new recruit production will occur on the second half of the year.

Month	Total Volume ($000)	Seasonal Slowdown	New Recruit Change	Adjusted Total Volume ($000)
Jan	$ 2,800.2			$ 2,800.2
Feb	2,818.1			2,818.1
Mar	2,835.3			2,835.3
Apr	2,867.0			2,867.0
May	2,898.1			2,898.1
Jun	2,928.4			2,928.4
Jul	2,958.1		$0.6	2,958.7
Aug	2,987.1		0.8	2,987.9
Sep	3,015.4	(150.8)	0.9	2,865.5
Oct	3,035.4	(151.8)	1.0	2,884.6
Nov	3,054.8	(152.7)	1.1	2,903.2
Dec	3,073.4	(153.7)	1.1	2,920.8
Total	$35,271.3	$(609.0)	$5.5	$34,667.8

CHAPTER 2

1. Converting fractions to decimal form requires dividing the numerator by the denominator:

$$1 \div 19 = .0526$$
$$3 \div 16 = .1875$$
$$18 \div 35 = .5143$$

2. Decimals are turned into fractions by treating the decimal as a numerator. The denominator is 1, followed by as many zeros as there are digits to the right of the decimal. Reduce to the lowest possible form by finding a number by which both sides of the fraction are divisible:

$$.25 = 25/100 \text{ or } 1/4$$
$$.68 = 68/100 \text{ or } 17/25$$
$$.555 = 555/1000 \text{ or } 111/200$$

3. To convert numerical information into narrative form, first decide what is the most significant conclusion.

a. One possible answer is: "One dollar of four expended for telephone expenses is estimated to be a personal call."
b. The significant factor is the contribution to total revenues made by the division: "One-fourth of total revenues were generated in the eastern division."
c. The *increase* in profit levels is significant: "This month's profits were one-fourth greater than the previous month's."

CHAPTER 3

1. To find a weighted average, first convert the total loan amount to fractional form:

$$32/114 + 82/114 = 114/114$$

The formula consists of two sides, one for each of the loans:

$$(32/114 \times 11.25\%) + (82/114 \times 6\%)$$

Multiply these sides and add:

$$3.1579 + 4.3158 = 7.4737\%$$

2. a. To find the average, add the three months together, and divide by 3:

$$\$82,380 + \$78,318 + \$72,450 = \$233,148$$
$$\$233,148 \div 3 = \$77,716$$

b. Percentage increase, October over September:

$$\$82,380 - \$78,318 = \$4,062$$
$$\$4,062 \div \$78,318 = 5.19\%$$

September over August:

$$\$78,318 - \$72,450 = \$5,868$$
$$\$5,868 \div \$72,450 = 8.10\%$$

October over August:

$$\$82,380 - \$72,450 = \$9,930$$
$$\$9,930 \div \$72,450 = 13.71\%$$

October over the average:

$$\$82,380 - \$77,716 = \$4,664$$
$$\$4,664 \div \$77,716 = 6\%$$

3. To compute the annualized rate of return, divide the rate by the number of months and multiply the answer by 12.

    a. $12\% \div 15 \times 12 = 9.6\%$
    b. $14\% \div 22 \times 12 = 7.6\%$
    c. $6\% \div 11 \times 12 = 6.5\%$

You can also use the factors given in the table included with this chapter:

    a. $12\% \times 0.800 = 9.6\%$
    b. $14\% \times 0.545 = 7.6\%$
    c. $6\% \times 1.091 = 6.5\%$

4. A part-year rate is computed by dividing the rate by 12, and multiplying the answer by the number of months.

    a. $9\% \div 12 \times 7 = 5.2\%$
    b. $12\% \div 12 \times 5 = 5.0\%$
    c. $14\% \div 12 \times 3 = 3.5\%$

You can also use the factors given in the table included with this chapter:

a. 9% × 0.583 = 5.2%
b. 12% × 0.417 = 5.0%
c. 14% × 0.250 = 3.5%

CHAPTER 4

1. Ratios can be expressed in one of three forms. First, calculate the change: divide 62,800 by the previous total of 51,011:

$$62,800 \div 51,011 = 1.23$$

Then convert to each form:

a. 123% (increase in unit sales)
b. 1.2 to 1 (more units sold than during the previous period)
c. 1.23 (units sold for this period when compared to the previous period)

2. Advertising costs have risen, so the newer cost is unfavorable when compared to the previous year. To compute, divide 35 cents (current cost) by 22 cents (prior cost):

$$35 \div 22 = 1.59$$

Then convert to each form:

a. 159% (higher cost)
b. 1.59 to 1 (dollars spent this quarter compared to the same quarter last year)
c. 1.59 (more dollars expended than during the previous year's fourth quarter)

3. Convert the change into a ratio form:

$$\$81,650 \div \$72,005 = 1.13$$

Then, using each ratio form:

   a. Net profits this year were 113% over the previous year.
   b. Profits were 1.1 dollars for every 1 dollar of profit earned in the previous year.
   c. Profits increased 1.13 times over the previous year.

   4. a. The current ratio is computed by dividing current assets by current liabilities:

$$186,550 \div 89,307 = 2.1 \text{ to } 1$$

   b. Turnover in working capital is computed by dividing sales by the difference between current assets and current liabilities:

$$1,745,800 \div (186,550 - 89,307) = 18.0 \text{ times}$$

   c. Debt/equity ratio requires dividing total liabilities by tangible net worth (total net worth less intangible assets):

$$234,907 \div (387,454 - 10,000) = 62.2\%$$

   d. Return on sales is expressed in percentage form, and is the result of dividing net profits by sales:

$$118,700 \div 1,745,800 = 6.8\%$$

CHAPTER 5

   1. The trend in production is favorable (assuming the rate of defects is under control). A typical brief statement:

   Average units per employee per shift increased 12.5% last year, and an additional 14.8% this year.

   2. Note that the level of $14,800 per representative was for the summer, while the current level is for a winter month. An analysis of prior years shows an average predictable drop between 30 and 35%. Based on this year's averages, you would expect December's total to be between $9,620 and $10,360. However, this year's came in at $11,300.

a. This is a favorable trend when adjusted for seasonal changes.
b. Typical statement:

> Based on historical drops in average sales per representative, this December's level was expected to be no greater than $10,360. However, the level was reported at $11,300, 9% above historical levels.

3. An analysis of the relative expense levels will reveal the following (as a percentage of sales):

Last year	70.4%
2 years ago	71.7
3 years ago	72.9
4 years ago	74.0

a. This is a favorable trend. Expenses are higher in amount each year, but as a percentage of sales, they are on a consistent decline.
b. Typical explanation:

> Expenses fell from 74.0% of sales to a stable level of 70.4% during the latest year.

4. Except for July, the current ratio for this company is falling consistently below 2 to 1 for the six-month period:

Jul	2.05 to 1
Aug	1.89 to 1
Sep	1.78 to 1
Oct	1.90 to 1
Nov	1.73 to 1
Dec	1.80 to 1

Investigate possible causes, such as:

1. The condition might be seasonal.
2. The problem might be chronic, caused by high current liabilities and lack of control over accounts receivable levels.
3. The current ratio could be at an acceptable level, given the nature

of the company and the industry; a more revealing trend might be found in the quick assets ratio (exclusion of inventories).

CHAPTER 6

1. The line graph should be scaled so that it can fit onto a half page of your report and at the same time enable the reader to recognize the significance of changes over time.

    a. A scale of 2,000 units per line will limit the height of the graph to 12 lines; 3,000 units per line reduces it to 8 lines.

    b. A 2-month time scale gives the graph 12 lines. However, an 8-line quarterly time summary better conforms to standard business reporting periods.

2. The full circle contains 360 degrees. Multiply the appropriate percentage by 360 to determine the right degree of each, and round your answer to the nearest full degree:

$$360 \times .47 = 169 \text{ degrees}$$
$$360 \times .34 = 123 \text{ degrees}$$
$$360 \times .19 = 68 \text{ degrees}$$

3. First, line up the protractor so that 0 and 180 degrees are level. Draw your first line from the center of the circle to the zero degree on the left. Find 169 degrees and draw a line from the center to that point. Then, using 169 as your new zero point, find 123 degrees, and draw a line to that point from the center. The last segment, from your last line to the original line you drew, will be 68 degrees. Refer to the circle chart example in Chapter 6.

CHAPTER 7

1. To construct a monthly interest rate table, first divide the annual rate by 12 to determine the monthly factor:

$$8\% \div 12 = .006667$$

Next compute each month's factor by multiplying 1 plus the factor by itself:

Month	Fraction	Factor
1	.006667	1.006667
2	.006667	1.013378
3	.006667	1.020135
4	.006667	1.026936
5	.006667	1.033782
6	.006667	1.040675
7	.006667	1.047613
8	.006667	1.054597
9	.006667	1.061628
10	.006667	1.068706
11	.006667	1.075831
12	.006667	1.083004

2. The time factor can be greater than one (when the period exceeds one year) or less than one (when the period is less than a full year).

a. In this example, 15 months is the equivalent of 1 1/4 years, or 1.25.

$$\text{Interest} = \$5,000 \times .07 \times 1.25$$
$$= \$437.50$$

b. Nine months represents 0.75 of a full year.

$$\text{Interest} = \$1,000 \times .06 \times 0.75$$
$$= \$45$$

c. Using the table in question 1, you find the interest portion for the full year (compounded monthly) is .083004.

$$\text{Interest} = \$800 \times .083004$$
$$= \$66.40$$

d. Simple interest involves no compounding. So the annual rate is multiplied by the number of years, two.

$$\text{Interest} = \$2,000 \times (.08 \times 2)$$
$$= \$320$$

e. In compounding, the annual rate must be multiplied by the periods involved. In this example, that is 1.06 × 1.06 × 1.06, or 1.06³.

$$\text{Interest} = \$1,000 \times 1.06^3$$
$$= \$191.02$$

3. The 360-day compound interest tables in the chapter give the factor for each of these problems.

a. 7.5% for 9 years: 1.9824

$$\$1,000 \times 1.9824 = \$1,982.40$$

b. 8.25% for 2 years: 1.1821

$$\$6,000 \times 1.1821 = \$7,092.60$$

c. 8% for 7 years: 1.7642

$$\$400 \times 1.7642 = \$705.68$$

4. The effective rate for annual compounding is a fraction of the full year's rate:

a. 2/12 of 11% = 1.83%
b. 3/12 of 11% = 2.75%
c. 8/12 of 11% = 7.33%

CHAPTER 8

1. Refer to the 9% Monthly Payment table in the chapter. The loan amount is shown down the far left-hand column. The number of years is listed across the top row:

a. $ 5,000 for 20 years: $ 44.99
b. $10,000 for 5 years: $207.59
c. $12,350 for 10 years: $156.47

The last answer must be calculated by adding together two factors from the table:

Payment on $10,000	$126.68
Payment on $1,000 (× 2)	25.34
Payment on $100 (× 3)	3.81
Payment on $50	.64
Total payment	$156.47

2. Begin by comparing total payments for 5 and 15 years, according to the amortization table, then calculate the total payment.

	5 years	15 years
Monthly payment	$ 103.80	$ 50.72
Total of payments	6,228.00	9,129.60
Less: loan amount	5,000.00	5,000.00
Interest expense	$1,228.00	$4,129.60

The savings is $2,901.60.

3. Begin looking up the required monthly payment on the interest amortization table: $76.01. (Add the payment on $5,000 to the payment on $1,000: $63.34 + $12.67 = $76.01.) To calculate each month's interest, multiply the outstanding balance at the beginning of the month by 1/12 of 9%, or .0075:

Month	Payment	Interest	Principal	Balance
				$6,000.00
1	$76.01	$45.00	$31.01	5,968.99
2	76.01	44.77	31.24	5,937.75
3	76.01	44.53	31.48	5,906.27

CHAPTER 9

1. Tables for the accumulated value of 1 are built by multiplying the interest rate, plus 1, by each preceding year's factor.

Year 1: 1.0625000
Year 2: 1.0625000 × 1.0625 = 1.1289063
Year 3: 1.1289063 × 1.0625 = 1.1994629
Year 4: 1.1994629 × 1.0625 = 1.2744293
Year 5: 1.2744293 × 1.0625 = 1.3540811

2. a. To accumulate $1,000 in five years, multiply by the factor given on the table to determine your annual deposit:

$$\$1,000 \times 0.1738906 = \$173.89$$

b. To prove the amount, multiply out at the given interest rate of 7%:

Year	Deposit	Interest	Balance
1	$173.89	$ 0	$173.89
2	173.89	12.17	359.95
3	173.89	25.20	559.04
4	173.89	39.13	772.06
5	173.89	54.04	999.99

3. The amount of monthly payment required is found by multiplying the loan amount by the factor in the column for the years allowed:

a. $32,850 × 0.0098473 = $323.48
b. $50,000 × 0.0080522 = $402.61
c. $ 5,333 × 0.0205165 = $109.41
d. $85,000 × 0.0076891 = $653.57

CHAPTER 10

1. Nominal yield is the stated rate of interest, and annual yield is the rate after computing compounded interest.

a. The stated rate is 6.25%.
b. To compute quarterly compounding, divide the stated rate by 4 (quarters), add 1, and multiply four times:

1.015625 × 1.015625 × 1.015625 × 1.015625 = 6.398% annual yield

2. To determine current yield, divide the amount of interest earned by the current market value:

$$\$80 \div \$1,040 = 7.69\% \text{ current yield}$$

3. The net profit of $825,400 includes $32,000 for profits from foreign exchange changes, and $122,000 in reduced taxes due to a carryover loss. Neither of these can be expected to repeat in future years. To calculate a comparable net return, subtract these from profits. This results in an adjusted profit of $671,400, or a net return of 6.97%.

CHAPTER 11

1. To support your proposal, collect cost information and pertinent history of the machine now in use. Compare the cost of the new machine and its estimated useful life, with the cost of maintenance and downtime now being experienced. Look for a trend toward increasing maintenance. Also discuss the type of machine. Was it designed for the present work load? What is the quality, compared with the model you have in mind? How much money will the company save by replacing the present machine, and how much time will be needed to recapture the investment?

2. The moving average will be one-third of the total sales for the current month and the previous two months. So for January, add November, December, and January; then divide by 3:

$$(\$743,650 + \$710,054 + \$714,371) \div 3 = \$722,692$$

Next, drop off the earliest month and add the newest. Following the same procedure, you can then compute each average. For the whole year:

January	$722,692	July	$924,337
February	741,588	August	957,175
March	767,705	September	964,054
April	812,892	October	917,819
May	840,312	November	859,559
June	880,846	December	807,193

3. There appears to be a seasonal swing in the volume of sales. If this is so every year, you should note it in your report. Also discuss changes in the market, customer base, and sales force, if applicable. Research levels of promotional expenses for the year, and relate significant increases and decreases to changes in the moving average.

Index